LAKE DISTRICT

30 HIGH LEVEL
AND FELL WALKS

by Vivienne Crow

JUNIPER HOUSE, MURLEY MOSS,
OXENHOLME ROAD, KENDAL, CUMBRIA LA9 7RL
www.cicerone.co.uk

© Vivienne Crow 2015
First edition 2015
ISBN: 978 1 85284 735 7
Reprinted 2017, 2019, 2021 (with updates)

Printed in China on responsibly sourced paper on behalf of Latitude Press Ltd
A catalogue record for this book is available from the British Library.
All photographs are by the author unless otherwise stated.

Acknowledgements

As a Lake District addict, I am always grateful to the many organisations – often dependant on the work of volunteers – that help make walking in the National Park as safe and as enjoyable as possible. These include the National Trust, the Lake District National Park, the Friends of the Lake District, Fix the Fells, various local authorities and, of course, the hard-working Mountain Rescue teams.

Also, I'd like to thank Heleyne and Jess for being such good company on many of the walks in this book, and Steve Ferrie for showing me that Striding Edge is nowhere near as scary as its reputation.

Updates to this Guide

While every effort is made by our authors to ensure the accuracy of guidebooks as they go to print, changes can occur during the lifetime of an edition. Any updates that we know of for this guide will be on the Cicerone website (www.cicerone.co.uk/735/updates), so please check before planning your trip. We also advise that you check information about such things as transport, accommodation and shops locally. Even rights of way can be altered over time. We are always grateful for information about any discrepancies between a guidebook and the facts on the ground, sent by email to updates@cicerone.co.uk or by post to Cicerone, Juniper House, Murley Moss, Oxenholme Road, Kendal LA9 7RL.

Register your book: To sign up to receive free updates, special offers and GPX files where available, register your book at www.cicerone.co.uk.

Front cover: Descending from Bow Fell with the Scafells in the background (Walk 19)

CONTENTS

A lovely but all-too-brief section of ridge on Longside Edge on the way up Skiddaw (Walk 1)

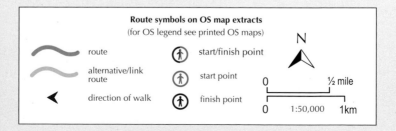

Route symbols on OS map extracts
(for OS legend see printed OS maps)

N

~~~ route

~~~ alternative/link route

◄ direction of walk

🚶 start/finish point

🚶 start point

🚶 finish point

0   ½ mile

0   1:50,000   1km

Area	Walk no	Walk	Start
Walks from the Keswick area	1	Skiddaw via Ullock Pike	Near Bassenthwai
	2	Blencathra and its neighbours	Mungrisdale
	3	Coledale Horseshoe	Braithwaite
	4	Newlands Round	Skelgill
	5	Causey Pike, Knott Rigg and Robinson	Newlands Valley
	6	Helvellyn range, end to end	Near Castlerigg
Walks from Borrowdale and Buttermere	7	Scafell Pike	Seathwaite
	8	Glaramara and Allen Crags	Stonethwaite
	9	Great Gable (from Honister)	Honister Pass
	10	Hay Stacks	Near Buttermere
	11	Grasmoor and Gasgale Crags	Crummock Wate
Walks from the Western Valleys	12	The High Stile ridge	Ennerdale
	13	Great Gable (from Wasdale Head)	Wasdale Head
	14	Pillar and Red Pike	Wasdale
	15	Scafell	Boot, Eskdale
Walks from Coniston and Langdale	16	The Coniston Fells	Coniston
	17	The Langdale Pikes	Great Langdale
	18	Pike o' Blisco and Crinkle Crags	Great Langdale
	19	Bow Fell and the Mickleden Round	Great Langdale
Walks from Ambleside, Grasmere and Windermere	20	Fairfield Horseshoe	Ambleside
	21	Helm Crag and Blea Rigg	Grasmere
	22	Kentmere Round	Kentmere
Walks from the Ullswater area	23	Helvellyn via the edges	Glenridding
	24	Deepdale Round	Patterdale
	25	Caiston Glen Round	Brothers Water
	26	Hartsop Dodd and Gray Crag	Hartsop
	27	High Street and Harter Fell	Haweswater
	28	A Martindale Round	Howtown
	29	Place Fell and Beda Fell	Patterdale
	30	Matterdale and The Dodds	Aira Force

Distance	Grade	Time	Page
17.4km (10¾ miles)	3	6½hrs	**24**
14km (8¾ miles)	3	5½hrs	**30**
14.8km (9¼ miles)	4	6½hrs	**36**
16.3km (10 miles)	3/4	6¾hrs	**42**
15.5km (9½ miles)	4	6½hrs	**48**
23.5km (14½ miles)	5	9hrs	**53**
14.5km (9 miles)	4	6hrs	**62**
17.4km (10¾ miles)	3/4	6¼hrs	**67**
8.9km (5½ miles)	2/3	4¼hrs	**73**
6.9km (4¼ miles)	1	3hrs	**79**
10.3km (6½ miles)	3/4	4½hrs	**83**
20.3km (12½ miles)	4	7½hrs	**90**
9.3km (5¾ miles)	3/4	5hrs	**96**
15.8km (9¾ miles)	4	6¾hrs	**101**
16.7km (10½ miles)	4	7hrs	**106**
19.6km (12¼ miles)	5	8hrs	**114**
12.1km (7½ miles)	2/3	5½hrs	**120**
11.9km (7½ miles)	3/4	6½hrs	**126**
14.8km (9¼ miles)	3/4	7½hrs	**131**
16.9km (10½ miles)	3	6½hrs	**138**
15.1km (9½ miles)	2	5¾hrs	**144**
19.5km (12 miles)	3/4	7¼hrs	**149**
12.9km (8 miles)	3/4	5hrs	**156**
15.5km (9½ miles)	3/4	5¼hrs	**162**
10.8km (6¾ miles)	2/3	4½hrs	**167**
9.5km (6 miles)	2/3	4½hrs	**173**
10.5km (6½ miles)	2	4½hrs	**178**
17km (10½ miles)	3	6hrs	**184**
12.9km (8 miles)	2/3	5½hrs	**190**
22.2km (13¾ miles)	3/4	7¾hrs	**196**

Dropping towards Eel Tarn on the descent from Scafell (Walk 15)

Bow Fell is one of the highest fells in the Lake District (Walk 19)

INTRODUCTION

To stride out along the crest of the fells and gaze down on sparkling lakes. To climb airy ridges with breathtakingly beautiful views. To witness the peregrine hunting down its prey or the raven performing its aerobatic tricks. To spend whole days exploring hanging valleys and hidden mountain tarns. This is what it means to walk in the most spectacular, the most beautiful scenery that England has to offer: the Lake District.

From its highest mountain tops and craggiest peaks to its loneliest ridges and most spectacular glacier-carved dales, this guide aims to seek out the best that the high Lake District fells have to offer. Those who are new to walking in this much loved corner

of the country will find relatively easy introductions to fell-walking, such as the route on to Hay Stacks (Walk 10), as well as the opportunity to head on to iconic mountains, including Scafell Pike (Walk 7) and Great Gable (Walks 9 and 13). Those who already know the National Park and UNESCO World Heritage Site, will enjoy a new take on Lakeland classics such as the Skiddaw linear (Walk 1) as well as a chance to explore less well-known areas, including Martindale (Walk 28). All the major horseshoe routes are here – including Kentmere, Coledale and Fairfield – and a few more besides.

Be warned though: walk the walks in this book and you'll want to come back for more. The Lake District is addictive. But with such a huge area to explore – a landscape that, although timeless, manages never to look the same from one day to another – there's a lifetime of fell-walking out there to feed your addiction.

GEOLOGY

The Lake District's rocks can be divided into six main types: Skiddaw slates, Borrowdale volcanics, Silurian slates, Coniston limestone, Carboniferous limestone and granite. They give rise to a surprisingly varied landscape for such a small area.

The Skiddaw slates are the oldest. Laid down by sedimentary processes almost 500 million years ago,

they give rise to generally smooth, rounded hills such as those of the Northern Fells. The Borrowdale volcanics were created about 450 million years ago. More resistant to erosion, they've created the high, craggy mountains of the central Lake District. Further south, the lower hills are made up of slates, siltstones and sandstones from the Silurian period, about 420 million years ago. Between the Borrowdale volcanics and the Silurian slates is a narrow band of limestone – known as Coniston limestone – stretching from the Duddon Estuary to Shap. Another area of limestone, dating from the Carboniferous period and often creating limestone pavement, or karst scenery, forms a partial ring around

Sharp Edge on Blencathra (Walk 2) is composed of sedimentary Skiddaw slates

An 'erratic' left by a retreating glacier

the edge of Cumbria, including the south-east corner of the Lake District. The final group of rocks are the granite intrusions that appear in just a few places, including Eskdale.

Periods of catastrophic earth movements, as continents have collided throughout the earth's history, have helped shape the Lake District. The mountain-building event known as the Variscan orogeny, for instance, created the broad dome that gives the Lake District National Park its basic profile. But it is the action of ice during the last glacial period, which ended about 10,000 years ago, that created most of the surface features we see today. The glaciers that formed in the central part of the Lake District produced a radial drainage pattern. They gouged out deep, U-shaped valleys and created arêtes, waterfalls in hanging valleys and long, narrow lakes held back by debris dropped by the retreating ice. High in the mountains, the ice plucked out corries, or cirques, that are now home to tarns.

WILDLIFE AND HABITATS

In spite of millions of years of geological upheaval, the Lake District is far from being a 'natural' landscape. The most common mammal you'll see on the walks in this book will be sheep. Mankind has been taming the mountains and valleys here for thousands of years. If they'd been left untouched, the fells would today be covered in a thick cloak of oak, birch and pine. Only the highest peaks would be visible, and the valleys would be impenetrable swamps.

That's not to say there are no native species left. Ancient woodland consisting largely of sessile oak still exists, while stands of birch and alder remain on the damp ground in some valley bottoms. There are also rowan, holly, crab-apple and witch-hazel as well as areas where Britain's only three native conifers – yew, juniper and Scots pine – can still be found.

Heathers, bilberry, lichen and mosses cover the fells, but there are wildflowers too in the woods and valley bottoms – red campion, lady's mantle, bog myrtle, spotted orchids, wood anemone, bog asphodel, bluebells and, of course, daffodils. Rare orchids can be found on the limestone pavement, as can some of Britain's most endangered butterflies, including the high brown and pearl-bordered fritillaries.

The fells are home all year round to ravens, buzzards and peregrines. Ospreys have recently returned to breed during the summer and red kites have also been reintroduced. (See Walk 26 for more on ravens and Walk 27 for birds of prey.) In the spring, you'll encounter a range of migratory species, including wheatear and ring ouzel on the fells and, lower down, redstart, pied flycatcher, wood warbler and tree pipit. Among the year-round valley residents are dippers, wagtails, chaffinches, great-spotted

Glencoyne Park (Walk 30)

Mosedale – a typical Lake District valley (Walk 14)

woodpeckers, nuthatches and sparrowhawks. With so many lakes, you'll inevitably come across large numbers of waterfowl too.

The Lake District's woods are home to roe deer, otters, badgers, voles, shrews, red squirrels, dormice and even the rare and elusive pine marten. You may occasionally catch sight of foxes, hares and stoats, while red deer tend to be confined to the higher fells (see Walk 29).

HISTORY

The first solid evidence of human existence in the county we now call Cumbria comes from the Mesolithic period, between 10,000BC and 4500BC. Tiny flint chippings have been unearthed on the coast, proof that these hunter-gatherers made it this far north. But it was really only in Neolithic times that human beings, farming for the first time, began to have a more profound impact on the landscape. Suddenly, after centuries of being left to their own devices, the forests that had slowly colonised the land after the departure of the last ice sheets were under threat as trees made way for crops and livestock.

Neolithic and, later, Bronze Age people left their mark on the Lake District landscape in other ways too – in the form of stone circles such as those at Castlerigg near Keswick and the Cockpit near Pooley Bridge.

The Iron Age, starting in roughly 800BC in Britain and lasting up until the arrival of the Romans, introduced more sophisticated farming methods as well as the Celtic languages that feature in topographical place names. *Blain* meaning summit, for example, gives rise to 'blen' as in Blencathra. The most dramatic remains of the Celtic people are their hill forts at places such as Castle Crag and Carrock Fell near Caldbeck.

When the Romans arrived in Britain in AD43, the Celtic people of northern England, the Brigantes, made pacts with the invaders and were allowed to live autonomously for many years. Eventually, though, the deals broke down as the Brigantes began fighting among themselves, and the new rulers moved in to quash them. (See Walk 28 for more on the Romans.)

As in most of Britain, little is known about the period after the Romans left. These are the Dark Ages, when fact and fiction become intertwined and semi-mythological figures such as King Arthur and Urien of Rheged appear. The latter, famed for uniting northern Celtic kings against the Anglo-Saxons, is thought to have ruled over much of modern-day Cumbria.

Celtic rule began to decline in the early seventh century and,

Coniston Old Man is littered with the remains of old quarries and mines (Walk 16)

before long, the Anglo-Saxons held power in much of lowland Cumbria. In the uplands, however, it was the Norsemen who dominated. These settlers, of Scandinavian origin, began arriving from Ireland and the Isle of Man towards the end of the ninth century. Like the Celts, they left their mark on the modern map of Cumbria: the word fell, for instance, comes from the Norse *fjell*, meaning mountain.

After the Norman conquest, Cumbria, like all of the border lands, entered a period of instability as territory passed from English rule to Scottish rule and back again. In the early part of the 14th century, Scottish raiders, led by Robert the Bruce, ransacked much of the county – towns were burned, churches destroyed and villagers slaughtered. During a particularly grim period in their history, Cumbrians also had to cope with famines, the Black Death and the infamous Border Reivers – the lawless clans that went about the region looting and pillaging. Life really only began to settle down in 1603 when James VI of Scotland became the first ruler of both England and Scotland. (See Walk 22 for more on the border troubles.)

Trade and industry played an important role in the development of the Lake District from the 13th century onwards when wealthy monastic houses, most notably the Furness Cistercians, made money from the wool trade, brewing and coppicing. The latter resulted in timber as well as charcoal destined for the area's bloomeries, the earliest type of furnace to smelt iron from its oxides. Mineral exploitation proper took off in the 16th century when Elizabeth I invited German miners to come to England. The scars of their industry – and the subsequent operations which reached their peak in the 19th century – still litter the Lake District.

The mining and quarrying industries weren't the only activities to take advantage of the Lake District's natural resources. The area's wealth of water, in the form of fast-flowing rivers and becks, allowed it to play a significant role in the textile industry too. While the wool industry, centred on Kendal, thrived from the 14th century onwards, during the Industrial Revolution the region's water-powered mills were providing bobbins for the huge cotton mills of Yorkshire and Lancashire. And, from the 18th century onwards, its landscape began generating money from tourism, a sector that got a big boost from the birth of the railways in the 19th century as well as a change in attitudes towards nature and the countryside.

The latter was partly inspired by the Romantic movement: the artists and poets who looked at the wild and rugged mountain scenery and saw something aesthetically pleasing rather than something to be feared. And, from this movement, came the desire to protect the natural world. The Cumberland-born poet William Wordsworth first put forward the idea of the Lake District as a 'national park' or, as he wrote, 'a sort of national property, in which every man has a right and interest who has an eye to perceive and a heart to enjoy'.

Later, the great Victorian thinker John Ruskin, who made his home on the shores of Coniston Water, was instrumental in the setting up of the National Trust. A passionate conservationist with a great love of the Lake District, he introduced Canon Hardwicke Rawnsley, vicar of Low Wray Church near Hawkshead, and later Crosthwaite in Keswick, to his friend Octavia Hill, a social reformer. The pair, together with lawyer Sir Robert Hunter, set up the National Trust in 1895, with the 108-acre Brandelhow estate on the western shore of Derwent Water becoming one of their earliest purchases.

WEATHER

Lying on Britain's west coast and subject to the whims of the prevailing south-westerlies coming in off the Atlantic, the Lake District experiences very changeable weather. There's no denying that Cumbria is wet – Borrowdale, in fact, holds the UK record for the highest rainfall in a 24-hour period – but that is only a fraction of the overall picture. The county is part of a windy, fast-moving scenario, which means the rain doesn't often linger. Spend a week in the Lake District, and you'd be unlucky if you had more than one day of heavy rain; sunshine and showers is more likely, and maybe even one or two days of brilliant blue skies.

Your best chance of dry weather is probably in May and June, but early spring and late autumn often hold some pleasant surprises too. As in the rest of the UK, the warmest weather is in June, July and August, although temperatures are lower than in the south of England. The coldest months are January and February, and this is when high road passes such as Kirkstone, Wrynose and Hardknott can become blocked by snow.

The weather is a very important consideration when heading on to the fells. Get an accurate, mountain-specific weather forecast before setting out, such as that provided by the Mountain Weather Information Service (www.mwis.org.uk). The Lake District Weatherline (0844 846 2444; www.lakedistrictweatherline.co.uk) has five-day Met Office forecasts and, during the winter, provides vital information on fell-top conditions, including depth of snow.

WHERE TO STAY

Tourism is a mainstay of the Lake District economy, so there's no shortage of beds, particularly at the middle and top end of the market. But the area's popularity means accommodation prices are relatively high. Budget travellers may want to consider youth

Looking out over Warnscale Bothy towards Buttermere and Crummock Water (Walk 10)

hostels or camping. You're also more likely to find good quality bed and breakfast accommodation at reasonable prices in the less well-known towns and villages, places such as Caldbeck at the base of the Northern Fells, Gosforth at the entrance to Wasdale and Ulverston in the south of the county.

However, if you do choose to stay in places such as these on the edge of the National Park, be aware that crossing the Lake District on narrow, winding roads, often using high mountain passes, can be a time-consuming business, particularly during the summer when the volume of traffic rises considerably.

The best bases for walks in this book are, inevitably, in the central honeypots, particularly Coniston, Grasmere, Ambleside and Keswick or, for walks in the east, Glenridding.

For detailed information on accommodation, the Lake District's tourist information centres are a superb resource (see Appendix A for details), as is the official website of Cumbria Tourism – www.visitlakedistrict.com.

GETTING AROUND

Contrary to popular myth, the Lake District's main towns, villages and dales are well served by buses, although a few routes run only

Using the Ullswater 'steamer' allows for linear routes (Walk 28)

in summer. Kendal, Windermere, Ambleside and Keswick are linked via the regular 555 service, which runs along the A591 through the middle of the Lakes. Other buses that may prove useful for accessing some of the walks in this book include the 508 serving the villages along the Ullswater shore; the handy 78 bus from Keswick, which runs through Borrowdale as far as Seatoller; the circular 77/77A summer-only route serving Keswick, Borrowdale, Honister, Buttermere, Lorton and Braithwaite; and the 505 from Kendal to Coniston via Ambleside. Relevant bus routes are listed in the information table at the start of each route. For some of the linear walks described, it is worth considering parking your car at the end of the walk, taking the bus to the start point and then walking back. That way, you eliminate the possibility of missing the last bus back.

No rail lines penetrate far into the National Park: a branch line from Oxenholme links Windermere with the West Coast Main Line, and the Cumbria Coast and Furness lines run along the county's coast, flirting briefly with the Lake District at Grange-over-Sands and Ravenglass. Eskdale is served by a miniature railway from Ravenglass – the Ravenglass and Eskdale Railway, affectionately known as the La'al Ratty.

Pick up a copy of Cumbria County Council's 'Travel Map and Guide' for basic information. Alternatively, phone Traveline on 0871 200 2233 or visit www.traveline.org.uk.

Regular ferry services on the main lakes – Derwentwater, Ullswater, Windermere and Coniston Water – are also a useful facility for walkers.

WAYMARKING AND ACCESS

In terms of waymarking and access, the Lake District is as close to heaven as walkers get in England. As well as thousands of kilometres of bridleways and footpaths, there are huge tracts of 'access land' – mostly mountains, moor, heath and common land where people can walk without having to follow rights of way. Stiles, bridges, gates and, in the valleys, fingerposts, are well maintained. Path surfaces too, which suffer erosion due to the combined effects of walkers' boots and wet weather, are looked after by a number of bodies. For more details on the Fix the Fells programme see Walk 3.

MAPS

The map extracts used in this book are from the Ordnance Survey's 1:50,000 Landranger series. They are meant as a guide only and walkers are advised to purchase the relevant map(s) – and know how to navigate using them.

The whole area is covered by sheets 89, 90, 96 and 97. The OS 1:25,000 Explorer series provides greater detail, showing field boundaries as well as access land. To complete all the walks in this guide using Explorer maps, you'll need sheets OL4, OL5, OL6 and OL7.

Harvey publishes an excellent series of Superwalker maps at the 1:25,000 scale. From 2015, its four Lakeland maps cover most of the National Park. It also publishes a 1:40,000 scale Lake District Mountain Map in conjunction with the British Mountaineering Council, which covers most of the main felltops.

CLOTHING, EQUIPMENT AND SAFETY

The amount of gear you take on a walk and the clothes you wear will differ according to the length of the route, the time of year and the terrain you're likely to encounter. Preparing for Scafell Pike in the height of winter, for example, requires more thought than when setting out to climb Helm Crag on a balmy spring afternoon.

Even in the height of summer, your daysack should contain everything you need to make yourself wind and waterproof. Most people carry several layers of clothing to cope with sudden changes in temperature and wind speed. As far as footwear goes, some walkers like good, solid leather boots with plenty of ankle support while others prefer something lighter.

Consider the changeable weather when preparing for the fells

Whatever you wear, make sure it has a good grip and isn't likely to result in a twisted ankle on uneven ground.

Every walker needs to carry a map and compass – and know how to use them. Always take food and water with you – enough to sustain you during the walk and extra rations in case you're out for longer than originally planned. Emergency equipment should include a whistle and a torch – the distress signal being six flashes/whistle-blasts repeated at one-minute intervals. Pack a small first aid kit too.

Carry a fully charged mobile telephone, but use it to summon help on the hills only in a genuine emergency.

If things do go badly wrong and you need help, first make sure you have a note of all the relevant details such as your location, the nature of the injury/problem, the number of people in the party and your mobile phone number. Only then should you dial 999 and ask for Cumbria Police, then mountain rescue. But remember that mobile reception is patchy in the Lake District.

DOGS

Dog owners should always be sensitive to the needs of livestock and wildlife. The law states that dogs have to be controlled so that they do not scare or disturb livestock or wildlife, including ground-nesting birds. On open access land, they have to be kept on leads of no more than 2m long from 1 March to 31 July – and all year round near sheep. A dog chasing lambing sheep can cause them to abort. Remember that, as a last resort, farmers can shoot dogs to protect their livestock.

Cattle, particularly cows with calves, may very occasionally pose a risk to walkers with dogs. If you ever feel threatened by cattle, you should let go of your dog's lead and let it run free, and move yourself to a safe place.

USING THIS GUIDE

The routes in this book cover the whole of the Lake District and are divided into six sections, depending on the most convenient base for the walk: Keswick; Borrowdale and Buttermere; the Western Valleys; Coniston and Langdale; Ambleside, Grasmere and Windermere; and the Ullswater area. (See the Route Summary Table for a comparison of

Looking back towards the Helvellyn range from the path to Codale Head (Walk 21)

The upper reaches of the Newlands Valley and, behind, the impressive High Stile range (Walk 5)

routes to help you choose the best walk for you.)

Most are circular, but there are a few linear walks that make use of the area's buses and boats. Check timetables carefully to make sure you have enough time to complete the route.

Each walk description contains information on start/finish points; distance covered; total ascent; grade; approximate walking time (not including time for rest breaks, taking pictures etc.); terrain; maps required; refreshments; and public transport options. The walks are graded one to five, one being the easiest. Please note that these ratings are subjective: based not just on distance and total ascent, but also the type of terrain encountered and the amount of scrambling, if any, that is involved. So, whereas the 'Place Fell and Beda Fell' route (walk 29) involves almost exactly the same distance and the same amount of ascent as 'Helvellyn via the edges' (walk 23), the latter is a grade higher because of the scrambling involved. Walkers are advised to read route descriptions in full before setting out to get a sense of what to expect. It might be an idea to do a grade one or two walk first and then judge the rest accordingly. The route summary table on pages 6 and 7 will help you make your choice.

WALKS FROM THE
KESWICK AREA

Looking back across the Newlands Valley to Skiddaw (Walk 5)

Walk 1
Skiddaw via Ullock Pike

Most people who climb Skiddaw, England's fourth highest mountain, use the constructed tourist path over Jenkin Hill. A far superior alternative is to combine the best way on to the 3054ft fell – via Ullock Pike and Longside Edge – with the best way down – via Sale How, Skiddaw House and the Glenderaterra valley. The result? The best Skiddaw walk...ever! It's a linear route that covers a vast variety of terrain, from steep, rocky ridge to rolling, heather-clad hills, with superb views of both sides of the mountain – and, at busy times, avoids the crowds on the tourist path.

Nearing Carl Side with Skiddaw up to the left

Start	Ravenstone Manor, near Bassenthwaite (NY 235 296)
Finish	Main bus stands in front of Booths Supermarket, Keswick (NY 263 235)
Distance	17.4km (10¾ miles)
Total ascent	965m (3170ft)
Grade	3
Walking time	6½hrs
Terrain	Rocky ascent; steep, loose material on one section; grassy fell, damp in places; valley tracks and paths; short section through town
Maps	OS Explorer OL4; or OS Landrangers 89 or 90
Refreshments	Choice of pubs and cafés in Keswick
Transport	Buses X4, 554 or 73/73A can be caught from Keswick to the start of the walk.

Catch the X4, 554 or 73/73A bus from Keswick and get off at Ravenstone Manor hotel, about 1.6km north of the main Dodd Wood car park. If you park at Dodd Wood, it'll take about 20–25mins to walk from the car park to Ravenstone Manor. There are two fingerposts just to the south of the hotel. One points south, back towards Dodd Wood, but you want the bridleway indicated by the other signpost: heading steeply uphill through the trees.

On reaching a grassed-over forest path, cross diagonally right to continue the climb. You soon go through a gate and step out into open country. Losing the trees on the left, Bassenthwaite Lake appears below and, in the distance, the misty outline of the Scottish hills fills the horizon.

Keep to the stony path as it swings away from the fence at a faint fork. On reaching the ridge – and your first view of Skiddaw's intimidating western slopes – bear right. It's a

The heart of the Northern Fells

relentless climb on to **Ullock Pike**, and the final part is the steepest – with some sections of bare rock to negotiate – but beyond the knobbly top, you are rewarded with a lovely, albeit brief section of high ridge walking ascending at a much gentler gradient. After the initial climb, you'll positively float along, delighting in the sparkling vision of Derwentwater to the south.

As the **Longside Edge** ridge broadens, peak-baggers may be interested in the faint path, to the right, on to **Carl Side**. The main route, however, skirts the northern flank of this grassy dome and then swings left to begin the toughest part of the climb.

The path pushes up through Skiddaw's very steep, very loose scree slopes. Gaining a good foothold on this unstable surface can be difficult in places; the best way to do it is to charge up at full pelt. With your calf muscles screaming for a rest, you eventually reach a cairn-cum-shelter on the summit plateau. Turn left here and savour the scene east across the Northern Fells towards the Pennines as you walk the last few metres to the trig pillar, shelter and viewfinder on the top of **Skiddaw**.

Of course, the views from **Skiddaw** are superb – this is England's fourth highest mountain, after all. It also benefits from standing at the edge of the Lake District National Park – with no other mountains of comparable stature to impede the outlook.

From the top, turn round and retrace your steps. Walk past the first shelter and, ignoring your ascent path, keep left to descend a badly eroded path and go through a gate. A few paces beyond the gate, turn left along a faint, grassy path. This heads east north-east, quickly veering north-east as it joins a slightly clearer route. The nature of the entire walk does an about-turn here. Gone are the harsh, imposing slopes of Skiddaw's west face, replaced now by a softer, more open and rounded outlook. Gone too are the rock and scree; there's now soft grass underfoot. If you want to cut short the route, keep to the main path beyond the gate, rejoining the walk description at the gate at the bottom of the tourist path.

The path drops into a boggy dip before ascending **Sale How**. With the ground getting wetter as you lose height, follow the path down the other side of this small, rounded hill. On reaching the boundary wall of **Skiddaw House**, keep it on your right and follow it round to a T-junction with a clear, broad track. Cross straight over to pick up a grassy path that swings right, beside the hostel's garden wall.

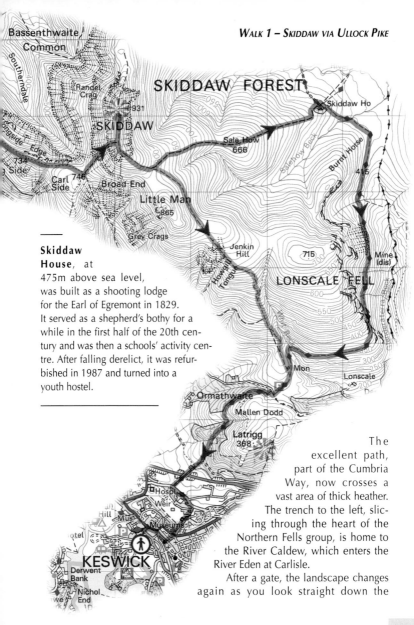

Skiddaw House, at 475m above sea level, was built as a shooting lodge for the Earl of Egremont in 1829. It served as a shepherd's bothy for a while in the first half of the 20th century and was then a schools' activity centre. After falling derelict, it was refurbished in 1987 and turned into a youth hostel.

The excellent path, part of the Cumbria Way, now crosses a vast area of thick heather. The trench to the left, slicing through the heart of the Northern Fells group, is home to the River Caldew, which enters the River Eden at Carlisle.

After a gate, the landscape changes again as you look straight down the

Glenderaterra gap. The path makes directly for the pyramid-like peak of Lonscale Fell and is soon accompanied by a wall on the left. As this swings away again, close to some ruined buildings, the path forks. Keep right – along the higher of the two routes. This climbs briefly before contouring the fellside, high above the **Glenderaterra Beck**, which has carved a narrow, steep-sided valley between Lonscale Fell and Blease Fell, the grassy, western edge of Blencathra. The ground on your left plummets steeply to the valley floor, more than 150m below, making your journey downstream an exciting one.

Just after a rocky section, you emerge from the valley to be greeted by an impressive panorama. From the left, the view includes Clough Head, High Rigg and Bleaberry Fell. As you pass through the next gate, Derwentwater also comes into view, as do the fells west of the lake.

The track crosses a lovely, tree-lined ravine through which **Whit Beck** flows, and then joins the Skiddaw tourist path at a gate. The alternative route rejoins the main route here.

The view from the valley of the Glenderaterra

Follow the wall on your right until you reach a large gate on the right. Go through this, walk along the rough road for about 70m and then go left, through a kissing-gate – signposted Keswick. Keep right at any forks as the well-used path steadily descends. It crosses the **A66** via a bridge and then reaches Briar Rigg on the edge of Keswick.

To return to the bus stands near Booths supermarket, turn left along this residential street. Go right at a small roundabout and then walk to the left of the leisure centre. Follow the path around the front of the building and out on to the road, along which you turn right. Continue past the **museum** and go straight over at the busy crossroads – along Station Street. When this bends sharp left, go right – soon passing the Moot Hall. When the pedestrianised area ends, keep straight ahead and then go left at the roundabout. Booths is on your right as this road then bends left.

Walk 2

Blencathra and its neighbours

*Mighty Blencathra (868m) is best known for its magnificent, spiky arêtes which
tower above the A66, bewitching drivers as they make their way from the M6
to Keswick. While providing walkers with some superb views of these ridges,
our route steers clear of their difficulties by approaching the mountain from the
east. It starts by climbing the lonely, grassy top of Bowscale Fell (702m) and
finishes on Souther Fell (522m). In between is the summit of Blencathra – a
wonderful place to linger on a clear day. The arêtes, the steep drops to the
south and the mountain's relative isolation give it a very airy, exposed feel.*

On Souther Fell with Bannerdale Crags behind and Blencathra in the distance

Start/finish	Parking area opposite Mungrisdale Village Hall (NY 363 302)
Distance	14km (8¾ miles)
Total ascent	900m (2950ft)
Grade	3
Walking time	5½hrs
Terrain	Mostly grassy fell, boggy in places; steep, stony ascent; short section of road walking
Maps	OS Explorer OL5; or OS Landranger 90
Refreshments	The Mill Inn at Mungrisdale
Transport	Bus 73/73A

Facing the village hall from the parking area, turn left along the road, which winds its way through Mungrisdale. Immediately after passing a road to Hutton Roof on your right, turn left along a rough lane. About 15m beyond a gate, leave the track by turning right – along a faint path to the left of the old quarry. Veering left, the trail becomes considerably steeper and looser as it rises through the spiky gorse. Thankfully though, the hard work is quickly over, and you are soon able to savour the views of the North Pennines and the Scottish hills as the trail becomes grassier and the incline gentler.

As the path swings west, up the broad shoulder of the fell, you may need to divert around some peaty patches, but in dry weather the ground is soft and springy. When you get your first view of Skiddaw to the west, the path veers west south-west as it dips slightly. A short detour to the edge of the fell to your right provides a glimpse of **Bowscale Tarn** in the bowl far below.

Head south-west out of the dip for the final, easy pull to **Bowscale Fell's** summit, marked by a cairn and, just beyond it, a shelter. Walk down

Bowscale Fell's eastern ridge

Blencathra's eastern face including Sharp Edge and Foule Crag

the other side of the fell, aiming for brooding Blencathra. There is some boggy ground ahead and it's best to stay left to avoid the worst of it. Having bypassed the largest pools, resume your south south-west line to rejoin a reasonable path. If you want to cut short the route, take the narrow path on the left about 400m beyond the summit of Bowscale Fell. From here, it's 3.2km back to Mungrisdale.

Dropping to the col at the head of the **River Glenderamackin**, keep straight ahead to climb on to **Blencathra**. The last section of the ascent, consisting of a steep, loose path, brings you to a cairn on the edge of the summit plateau.

To reach the true summit, you now have a choice. The main route heads left, following the very edge of the fell and losing a little height to look down on to **Sharp Edge**. Dropping down to the narrow path around the edge of the fell, you get a bird's eye view of the bare rock of this famous scramble. At the top of it, bear right and, with views of Scales Tarn far below, head for the summit, known as **Hallsfell Top**. Alternatively, from the cairn on the edge of the plateau, head right (south) and follow a faint path past a cross and a small pool to reach the top.

From the summit, head east north-east for 150m – back the way you came if you chose the main route to the summit – and then bear right at a fork to begin the zig-zagging descent down the constructed path. About 1.4km from the summit, leave **Scales Fell's** gorgeous ridge path by bearing left at a faint fork (east north-east at first). Go straight across the clear path at the bottom of the slope and then, in 160m, join a track from the left. In another 200m, turn left, away from the main path, to climb **Souther Fell** (north-east, veering north north-east).

Ghost stories abound in the Lake District, one of the most famous of which involves Souther Fell. It was here, on Midsummer Eve in 1735, that William Lancaster's servant saw a troop of ghostly horsemen crossing the fell. Exactly a year later, Mr Lancaster and his family saw the same sight. All were ridiculed when they told of the huge numbers involved, ascending a stretch of the fell no rider would attempt and having found no sign of horses passing that way.

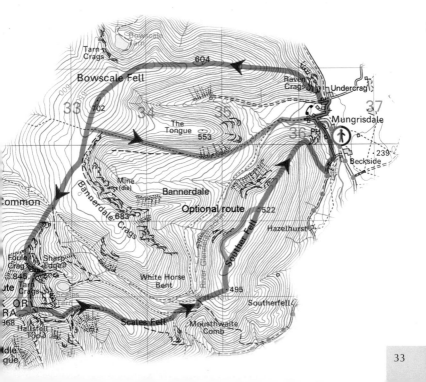

Looking down on Scales Fell

You soon reach the flat, damp top. Bear right at the fork to keep to the main path. Alternatively, bear left along a loop path that takes you out to a cairn on the western edge of the fell for good views across Bannerdale. This then rejoins the main path.

The highest point on Souther Fell is distinguished by a tiny rock outcrop on an otherwise grassy summit. Continuing in the same direction, it isn't long before the path begins dropping off the fell's north-eastern end.

A few paces beyond a rocky section, bear right along a narrow, easy-to-miss trail that cuts across the fellside, slowly losing height. On the way down, you'll encounter a fence. Follow this until it meets a gated road near some conifers. Turn left.

Take the narrow path on the right just before the Mill Inn and cross the footbridge over the River Glenderamackin to return to the parking area.

Walk 3

Coledale Horseshoe

The Coledale Horseshoe, probably the best round in the northern Lakes, takes in Barrow (455m), Sail (773m), Crag Hill (839m), Hopegill Head (770m) and Grisedale Pike (791m). Starting from the village of Braithwaite, it makes for a relatively long, hard day, but there are some magnificent views to be had almost from the outset; and, of course, there's that wonderful feeling of being totally immersed in the mountains as you follow long ridge lines on either side of the steep-sided valley carved by Coledale Beck.

The path up to the saddle between Causey Pike and Sail

Start/finish	Royal Oak pub in Braithwaite, near Keswick (NY 231 236). Parking can be found, outside of school hours, in the nearby school car park; alternative roadside parking in village
Distance	14.8km (9¼ miles)
Total ascent	1185m (3880ft)
Grade	4
Walking time	6½hr
Terrain	Mostly ridge walking; steep, rocky ascent of Crag Hill; loose, stony descent from Grisedale Pike; short sections of road walking
Maps	OS Explorer OL4; or OS Landrangers 89 or 90
Refreshments	Royal Oak, Middle Ruddings, Coledale Inn, Hobcartons tea room and Scotgate Holiday Park's tea room, all in Braithwaite
Transport	Buses X5 and summer-only service 77/77A

Standing on the main road through the village, with your back to the pub, turn left and immediately left again along a narrow lane through Braithwaite. After the last house on the right – about 150m after a small shop – turn right up the driveway to Braithwaite Lodge. Head to the right of the house and go through a gate behind some outbuildings. Follow the path up a small field and through a smaller gate in a wall. Bear left to reach the base of the ridge.

The famous **Cumberland Pencil Company**, established in 1868, was originally located in Braithwaite. The company only moved to Keswick at the end of the 19th century when the Braithwaite factory was destroyed by fire. It recently moved to the west coast, although its museum is still in Keswick.

Turn right on a grassy path that follows the crest of the ridge with widening views as you climb. The path takes you directly to the summit of **Barrow**. There are grand views all the way, especially back to Skiddaw and across the Newlands Valley to Cat Bells.

From Barrow's summit, the ridge path drops to Barrow Door, the gap between Barrow and the little summit of Stile End. Bear left (west south-west) here and, having ignored several lesser trails, you eventually meet the clear path coming up Stonycroft Gill from the left. The well-trodden route later curves left as you climb a narrower and steeper section of path. The ground can be loose here, with steep drops to the right, so watch your footing! It'll be quite a relief to reach the saddle between Causey Pike and Sail.

Having rested and enjoyed the superb views south, including the High Stile range, turn right to climb a constructed zig-zagging path up **Sail**. From the top, drop to a slender saddle between Sail and Crag Hill.

FIXING THE FELLS

Most of the constructed paths encountered on the Coledale Horseshoe are the end product of the Fix the Fells project. Working with rangers from the National Trust and the Lake District National Park, as well as dozens of volunteers, the scheme repairs upland paths throughout the Lake District.

With the erosive effects of millions of pairs of walkers' boots every year combining with a climate that is, to say the least, wet, the most walked areas of the National Park get quite a battering. With fell-walking increasing in popularity, moorland paths that were once pleasant, grassy trails can become deep, boggy trenches; vegetation can be stripped from huge swathes of ground; and paths on steep ground can be reduced to little more than scree runs. Such erosion not only makes the paths uncomfortable and even potentially dangerous for people to walk on, it also results in more sediment being washed into the area's rivers and lakes. This, in turn, affects water quality and wildlife. Since the project was set up earlier this century, Fix the Fells has been responsible for repairing and maintaining more than 200 paths. It uses a variety of techniques including stone pitching, soil inversion and 'floating paths' made from sheep's wool. The path leading down to Coledale Hause is one of the project's many success stories. It's hard to believe it now, but there used to be an erosion scar here – gouged out by rainwater – that was a couple of metres deep. But then Fix the Fells came along and carried out drainage work, constructed a path using sub-soil and filled in the ugly trench. Visit www.fixthefells.co.uk for details on how to donate or volunteer.

A prominent, constructed path on the eastern slopes of Sail

The climb up from the saddle is a little more interesting and challenging than the previous ascents of the day. Sometimes on bare rock, you may need to use your hands on the way to the top of **Crag Hill**. There are good views of the whole of the horseshoe from the trig pillar and, although you are now at the highest point on the walk, you can clearly see there's a lot more climbing to come.

There are two routes leading away from the summit. Take the more prominent one to the left (south-west). At the bottom of the slope, take the clear path on the right. Those walkers wanting to add Grasmoor to today's tally of summits should continue straight on from the bottom of the slope and then retrace their steps after visiting the summit. About 1km after the junction at the base of Crag Hill, turn left at a cairn on to a narrower path. If you want to cut short the route, keep straight on at the cairn and pick up the path into Coledale. It is then about 5km along the valley back to Braithwaite.

Bearing right at the next fork, you meet up with a path coming in from your right at boggy **Coledale Hause**. You'll now see two paths climbing from the pass (known in the Lake District as a hause). The one to the right (north-east) cuts the

corner and rejoins the main route on
the ridge at the eastern end of
Hobcarton Crag. However, it
would be a

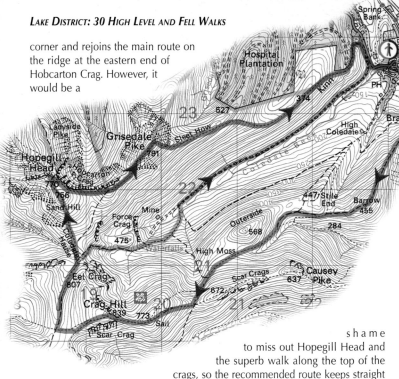

shame
to miss out Hopegill Head and
the superb walk along the top of the
crags, so the recommended route keeps straight
ahead (north) and climbs directly up **Sand Hill**.

Scree-covered, the ascent looks pretty tough from the bottom, but it's all over
in a flash and you soon encounter level ground. Just a few more strides and you're
at the airy summit of **Hopegill Head** – a great place for taking in the views and
simply enjoying the mountain air.

From the top, retrace your steps for about 100m and then bear left to follow the gently descending path along the rim of the fell. It's hard to resist going
to the edge and peering down on to the dark pinnacles and crags of awesome
Hobcarton Crag below.

The ridge path dips twice before the final big climb of the day – up to
Grisedale Pike. The summit consists of a rocky outcrop to the left of the path.
Dropping down from the summit, make sure you bear right at some rusty fenceposts in about 70m. The route is not obvious in misty conditions. The descent is
uncomfortable at first. You have to pick your way carefully down the shattered
rock on a badly eroded path, keeping your eyes firmly on the ground ahead. After

a slightly easier section, the path drops right – away from the main ridge and on to a lower, grassier spur.

In an attempt to control erosion on this popular fell, National Trust rangers have placed a wooden barrier across a route down to the right. Keep straight ahead here, rejoining the main path a little further down. Ignoring a narrow trail to the right, cross a stile in a fence. Keep to the main path, avoiding any shortcuts through the bracken, and you'll eventually reach the B5292. Turn right and follow the road back into Braithwaite.

On Sand Hill, looking back towards Eel Crag

Walk 4

Newlands Round

*The Newlands Round is another superb roller-coaster of a horseshoe.
Striding out along high, breezy ridges with far-reaching views
throughout, you'll take in Cat Bells (451m), Maiden Moor (576m),
High Spy (653m), Dale Head (753m) and Hindscarth (727m). There
are lots of ups and downs along the way and the terrain includes some
clambering on bare rock, so it's a reasonably tough undertaking – but
one that should leave you with some magnificent fell memories.*

The well-used path on to Cat Bells

Start/finish	Small car park near Skelgill, about 3.2km S of Portinscale (NY 246 211)
Distance	16.3km (10 miles)
Total ascent	1185m (3540ft)
Grade	3/4
Walking time	6¾hrs
Terrain	Mostly ridge walking; some bare rock on initial climb and descent from Hindscarth
Maps	OS Explorer OL4; or OS Landrangers 89 or 90
Refreshments	Swinside Inn in nearby Swinside
Transport	The summer-only bus 77/77A passes close to the start of the walk. The Keswick Launch across Derwentwater also serves nearby Hawes End (017687 72263 or www.keswick-launch.co.uk

Follow the path climbing from the eastern end of the car park – signposted Cat Bells. The early view of Skiddaw to the left is rather distracting, but there's more to come. As the main route swings right at a fork to begin climbing the ridge, Derwentwater and its many islands appear – a wonderful, sparkling scene.

The dramatic Dalehead Crags seen from High Spy

The path, clear on the ground, continues uphill. At the first rocky section – with its memorial to Thomas Arthur Leonard, founder of the 'open-air movement' – it is best to head left to avoid polished, slippery rock. Soon after this, the going gets a little easier for a short while.

The **respite** from the climb provides an opportunity to take in your surroundings at a more leisurely pace: to the left is Derwentwater, while the views to the right are dominated by the mountains surrounding the gorgeous Newlands Valley.

The path dips slightly before climbing again – at an even steeper angle than before. This section involves one short, easy rock clamber, and, once you've surmounted this difficulty, the summit cairn of **Cat Bells** is only a few metres further on.

From the top, continue along the clear path, which quickly drops to a junction in the hause between Cat Bells and Maiden Moor. Continue straight ahead. The climb on to **Maiden Moor** from here is not as steep as the route on to Cat Bells, but it can seem a bit of a plod after earlier exertions.

As the gradient eases and you get your first decent

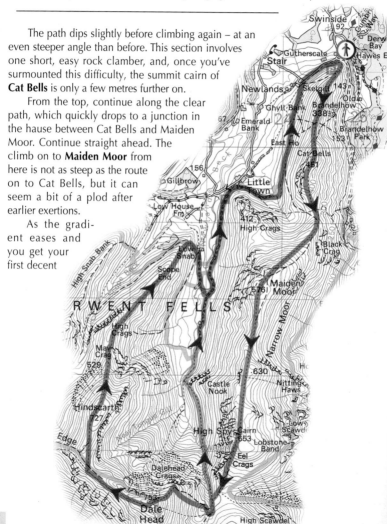

views south, turn right along a less well-walked path partly hidden by the rocky outcrop beside the path. Most walkers keep sheep-like to the main path that cuts uninspiringly across the dull moorland top, but our route heads over to the western edge for some superb views. It's mostly on grass, providing a welcome respite from the eroded ridge path. At one point, you crest a small rise and can see High Spy, Dale Head and Hindscarth ahead: the three remaining summits on the round.

Eventually, you rejoin the main path to climb to **High Spy**. Ignore trails to the left close to a sprawling cairn; simply keep to the wide route all the way to the tall, neat cairn marking the summit.

The **view south** opens out dramatically now – straight ahead is the highest ground in England, including the Scafells, Bow Fell, Great Gable and Great End.

From the 653m High Spy, you lose about 160m of height before having to climb all the way up to Dale Head – at 753m, the highest point on the walk. But what's a bit of knee-crunching descent in such magnificent surroundings? There are the dark crags of Dale Head's north-facing slopes over to the right and, later,

Walkers lose some height on the way down to Dalehead Tarn's outlet stream

On Hindscarth

lovely little Dalehead Tarn is visited. As you drop, don't be tempted by a cairned route to the left. The descent ends at a beck, which can be easily forded in all but the worst weather. If you want to cut short the route, a path follows the beck downstream and rejoins the main route after it crosses the beck near Low Snab farm.

After fording the beck, a constructed path leads to **Dalehead Tarn**. Keep the water on your left and pick up the path on to Dale Head. The climbs on to Cat Bells and Maiden Moor will seem like a walk in the park compared with this: it's very steep. And, just when you think it's all over – as you reach the top of the constructed path – you look to the left and realise the summit is still some way off.

From the top of **Dale Head**, the ridge path heads roughly north-west. The views south and west now take in Fleetwith, Kirk Fell, Pillar, the High Stile range and Buttermere. Just as the path begins to climb out of a grassy saddle, turn right. This easy-angled trail climbs to **Hindscarth**, joining a path from the left along the way.

From the summit, drop to a large shelter, from where the descent proper begins. The ground is loose and stony at first, but the gradient eventually eases and you find yourself on a pleasantly narrow, heathery ridge with views of the Coledale fells to the north-west. The way down then steepens again and you have a few straightforward rock steps to negotiate. Reaching a fence/wall, bear right to drop into the valley, passing beneath some spoil heaps on the way.

The **mines** on Cat Bells and in the Newlands Valley were first worked by Keswick's German miners. The Germans, at that time the best miners in Europe, were invited to England by Elizabeth I in 1564. Employed by the Company of Mines Royal, they established copper and lead mines throughout Cumbria, the centre of operations being Keswick.

On reaching a track close to **Low Snab farm**, turn right, signposted Dalehead. In about 150m, drop left and cross the footbridge. A few metres of grassy path leads to a wide track, along which you turn left.

After about 1km of track walking, bear right along a wide, gently rising grass path. Turn right at the next track junction. Ignoring a path to the right, follow the track down to some mine workings. After crossing a bridge, keep right at the fork. You're soon back on a clear track following the line of the intake wall. Turn right on reaching the road at Skelgill. It's now about 400m back to the car park.

Walk 5

Causey Pike, Knott Rigg and Robinson

There's nowhere quite like the North-Western Fells for ridge walking. Stand on any of the high summits in this area and you'll see layer upon layer of ridge: Whiteless Edge, the top of Gasgale Crags, Barrow, Hindscarth Edge, even lowly Cat Bells. This route stitches just a few of them together, dipping into and out of valleys and high passes along the way, to form a grand outing that takes in Rowling Edge to Scar Crags via Causey Pike; Ard Crags and Knott Rigg; and Robinson's north-east ridge. There are one or two exciting climbs along the way, as well as several opportunities to feel the wind in your hair as you walk the crest of the fells. The descent from Robinson involves a couple of tricky rock steps.

The scene from Causey Pike includes Knott Rigg and Robinson, both visited later in the walk

Start/finish	Parking area SW of Little Town in the Newlands Valley (NY 232 194)
Distance	15.5km (9½ miles)
Total ascent	1225m (4010ft)
Grade	4
Walking time	6½hr
Terrain	Quiet lane and farm paths early on; ridges and valleys; some steep ascents and descents, including easy scrambling; one boggy section; paths indistinct in places
Maps	OS Explorer OL4; or OS Landrangers 89 or 90
Refreshments	Little Town Farm has a tearoom and licensed bar; otherwise, the nearest pub is the Swinside Inn in Swinside.
Transport	None

Walk north-east along the road from the parking area. Skiddaw appears straight ahead, but take some time to look to the left too – to the distinctive little summit looming over the valley. That's Causey Pike, our first main top of the day.

After about 1.5km, you reach **Ghyll Bank**. Take the path through the small gate on the left immediately after the buildings. Cross the bridge at the bottom of the slope and then head up the path on the other side, to the right of a group of cottages. Go through a small gate, cross the cottages' driveway and continue uphill to the road.

Turn right, walk along the asphalt for about 50m and then step up on to the gently rising path to the left. On encountering a stony path coming up from the house below, bear left. Before long, this narrower path swings left and begins a steep, sometimes rocky

On the Knott Rigg and Ard Crags ridge

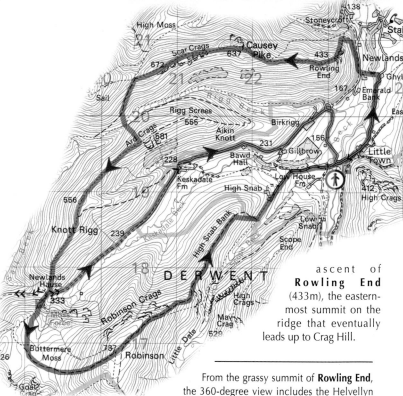

ascent of **Rowling End** (433m), the eastern-most summit on the ridge that eventually leads up to Crag Hill.

From the grassy summit of **Rowling End**, the 360-degree view includes the Helvellyn range, Dale Head, Hindscarth, Robinson, High Stile, Red Pike, Grisedale Pike, Skiddaw, Blencathra and the North Pennines.

The path continues through the heather and, before you know it, you're climbing again – on to **Causey Pike** (637m). This too is a steep ascent, rising to a rocky crescendo at the summit dome. You'll need your hands to haul yourself up the last section of this exhilarating scramble.

At the top, the **skyline** view takes in Scafell Pike and Scafell, but it's the scene to the south-west that is most captivating: taking in Pillar, the High Stile ridge, Robinson and, in the foreground, our next target, Ard Crags (581m).

The steep slopes of High Stile above Buttermere seen from Robinson

Continue along the clear ridge path, up and over **Scar Crags** and down into a pronounced dip at the base of the constructed path on to Sail. Look to the left and you'll see two paths. Take the further right of these (south south-west at first). As you descend, look across to the slope opposite and you'll see a faint path heading straight up the grassy hillside. That's our way on to Ard Crags. About 500m after leaving the ridge, turn left along an indistinct, grassy trail, which later follows a tiny beck downstream. On reaching a clearer path at the bottom of the slope, turn right to cross the beck, but then immediately go left along a narrow path. This is the ascent route seen from the other side of the valley. The good news is that it's not as steep as it looked from above.

The path leads directly on to the **Ard Crags** ridge, along which you turn right. Considering its rather meagre altitude, this makes for excellent walking – with good views ahead to the High Stile ridge and down into the steep-sided valley carved by Sail Beck. The ridge briefly broadens as it crosses the top of **Knott Rigg** (556m) and then narrows again as it drops to the road at **Newlands Hause**. To cut short the route, walkers could simply head left along the road and then turn right just before Rigg Beck to return to Little Town.

You'll see two paths heading south from the parking area in the pass. The one on the left heads into the confines of the gill for a view of Moss Force, worth the detour after heavy rain; but you need to take the one on the right, heading steeply uphill.

At the top of the ascent, keep right along a grassy path. After about 100m, bear left at a faint fork, heading south-west at first. The path weaves about as it negotiates the boggy ground of **Buttermere Moss**, but the general direction is south. After about 400m of bog-trotting, head left (east) to pick up a clearer path making its way towards **Robinson's** west-facing slopes. Choose your line carefully, but don't hang around – the moss is reluctant to give up any boots which linger for long. Only as you reach steeper ground does the going become firmer. The path gets steeper and stonier as it swings north-east to reach the summit.

The combination of exhaustion from having already climbed about 1200m and the wonderful view will keep you glued to the summit of **Robinson** for some time. The long, rocky ridge from Great End to Scafell is particularly absorbing, although Great Gable just blocks Scafell Pike's summit from view.

From the small shelter at the summit, walk north-east across the bare plateau. Finding the path off the fell could be difficult in misty conditions: if you're struggling, head slightly further east to pick up a cairned route that leads to the edge of the plateau. As soon as the descent begins, the path becomes clearer.

There are one or two loose, stony areas before you reach two rock steps that involve some scrambling. The lower step is the more awkward. Once the tricky bits are out of the way, you can relax and enjoy the next 1km stroll along the grassy crest of **High Snab Bank**. Approaching the end of the ridge, the path forks; bear right, continuing in the same direction, but no longer on the ridge top. The path then swings right to begin a steep descent on grass.

Turn left at the bottom of the slope and walk between two drystone walls. After passing to the right of a cottage, follow the access lane downhill to the road – passing tiny **Newlands Church** along the way. Turn right and the parking area is a few metres further on.

Walk 6
Helvellyn range, end to end

Stretching from Clough Head (726m) in the north to Dollywaggon Pike (858m) in the south and taking in Helvellyn (950m) along the way is a superb 12km-long ridge that never drops below 600m – probably one of the best and longest stretches of sustained high-level walking in the entire Lake District. Other summits climbed include Great Dodd (857m), Watson's Dodd (789m), Stybarrow Dodd (843m), Raise (883m) and Nethermost Pike (891m). There is a fair bit of road and track walking at the start to overcome the transport difficulties associated with linear walks, but the reward is a long and wonderful day on the high fells.

The broad, grassy ridge linking The Dodds

Start	Start of lane heading NE from Dale Bottom, near Castlerigg (NY 295 217). It is probably best to park near the AA box at Dunmail Raise and then catch the bus N along the A591 to Dale Bottom.
Finish	Dunmail Raise (NY 329 111)
Distance	23.5km (14½ miles)
Total ascent	1475m (4830ft)
Grade	5
Walking time	9hrs
Terrain	Quiet lanes and tracks; high ridge path; mixture of damp and stony ground; rocky gill on descent
Maps	OS Explorers OL4 and OL5; or OS Landranger 90
Refreshments	Travellers' Rest pub near Grasmere
Transport	Bus 555

From Dale Bottom, walk along the lane signposted to St John's in the Vale Church, quickly passing a campsite. Just after a gate on the road, turn left at a T-junction – towards **Sykes**. In about 600m, turn right up a rough track. As the track becomes surfaced again, you will pass the church. Keep to the lane as it heads downhill through a gate and then bends sharp right near **Yew Tree Farm**. Turn right at the next road junction, right again at the **B5322** and then left almost immediately – towards Matterdale.

Ignore a track to the right near some farm buildings early on. Having

passed through some gates along the way, you reach more open country and the track climbs to a crossing of ways. Keep straight ahead – uphill through the disused quarry with good views

Swirral Edge from the top of Helvellyn

across to Blencathra. You begin climbing with a fence on your right just after passing through a gate. Continue for 800m beyond this gate and then, as you reach the brow of the hill, go through a gate on the right. If you reach a tin-roofed building to the left of the track, you've gone too far and need to backtrack about 50m.

A moderately steep, narrow path heads up the grassy slope (south-west, swinging south). At the top of the first rise, you have the cairn-topped mound of White Pike to your left. Bear right to continue climbing to the summit of **Clough Head**.

The summit is marked by a **trig pillar**, with views of practically all the major fells to the west of the A591: from the Coniston range in the south, through Crinkle Crags and Bow Fell to the Scafell group and then on to Great Gable, the Newlands fells, the mountains around Coledale and, to the north, Skiddaw. On a clear day, even the mountains of Dumfries and Galloway are visible across the Solway Firth.

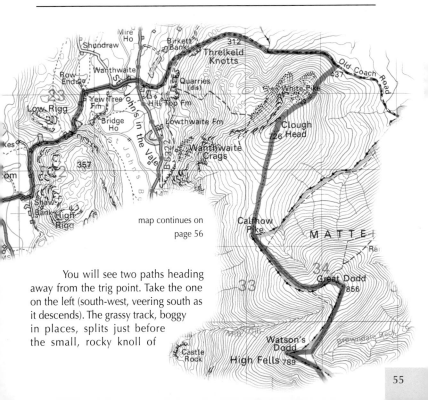

map continues on
page 56

You will see two paths heading away from the trig point. Take the one on the left (south-west, veering south as it descends). The grassy track, boggy in places, splits just before the small, rocky knoll of

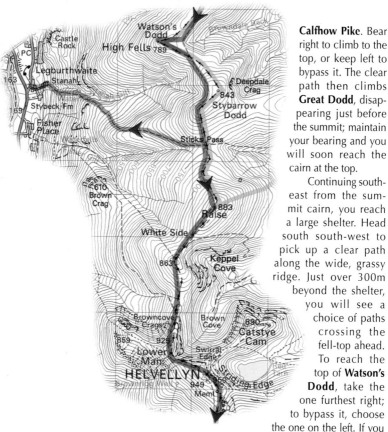

Calfhow Pike. Bear right to climb to the top, or keep left to bypass it. The clear path then climbs **Great Dodd**, disappearing just before the summit; maintain your bearing and you will soon reach the cairn at the top.

Continuing south-east from the summit cairn, you reach a large shelter. Head south south-west to pick up a clear path along the wide, grassy ridge. Just over 300m beyond the shelter, you will see a choice of paths crossing the fell-top ahead. To reach the top of **Watson's Dodd**, take the one furthest right; to bypass it, choose the one on the left. If you go out to the summit cairn, you will need to follow the grassy path south-east to regain the main route.

The clear track now swings south south-east to climb **Stybarrow Dodd**. It misses the summit cairn – which is a few metres to the left – and swings south-west. As you reach a cairn on the western edge of the ridge, the path seems to disappear. However, if you walk a few paces south from here, you will quickly pick up a stony path that drops to a crossing of routes in **Sticks Pass**. To cut the route short, walkers could turn right at the pass and descend to the road, catching the 555 bus from the junction of the B5322 and A591.

A clear path climbs beyond the pass to the stone column on top of **Raise**.

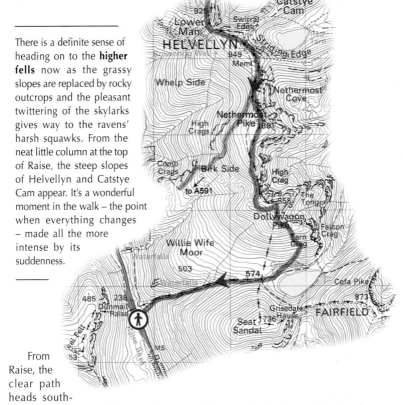

There is a definite sense of heading on to the **higher fells** now as the grassy slopes are replaced by rocky outcrops and the pleasant twittering of the skylarks gives way to the ravens' harsh squawks. From the neat little column at the top of Raise, the steep slopes of Helvellyn and Catstye Cam appear. It's a wonderful moment in the walk – the point when everything changes – made all the more intense by its suddenness.

From Raise, the clear path heads south-west and drops to a shallow saddle where it is joined by the Keppel Cove track from the left. There is now a short climb to **Whiteside**, before a narrower ridge leads more steeply on to **Lower Man**. At the top, you'll be able to see, for the first time, the entire ridge laid out behind you.

Bear left to make your way to the top of **Helvellyn**, England's third highest mountain. From the trig pillar and cairn, drop to the large shelter and then stick to the eastern rim of the mountain to peer down on to Red Tarn far below and the scramblers strung out along vertiginous Striding Edge. Just after the Gough Memorial, don't be tempted by the path dropping left to the arête. When the rim trail runs out, continue along the edge to rejoin the main path. Where it forks, bear left. For another way to cut short the route, walkers could turn right at this first fork to descend to the A591.

The path quickly forks again. Bear left here to climb to the top of **Nethermost Pike** and **High Crag**, enjoying superb, airy views from the fell edge. Alternatively, keep right to bypass the summits. The narrower trail along the edge later rejoins the main path, which dips just before **Dollwaggon Pike**. Where it forks, you again have a choice: bear left for the summit or keep right to bypass it. The narrower trail on to the pike rejoins the main path just as it begins to descend steeply.

With the summit of Helvellyn in sight, the path climbs Lower Man

The path down to **Grisedale Tarn** is steep, but most of it is pitched – thanks to the work of the Fix The Fells project (see Walk 3). As you near the tarn – on a bend to the left – leave the well-walked path by turning right along a faint, grassy trail (south-west). Damp in places, this passes over the top of a small rock outcrop and makes its way towards the western end of the tarn. You may well lose it along the way. If you do, look up to Seat Sandal straight ahead, and you will see a

Nearing Dollywaggon Pike, the final summit of the day

tumbledown wall coming down its northern face. This ends just before the bottom of the slope, but if you imagine it continuing in a straight line, the point at which it would reach the base of the slope is the point at which you will pick up a clearer path. Turn right along this (west south-west).

If you're feeling tired after your ten summits of the day, spare a thought for the fell-runners attempting the **Bob Graham Round**. In addition to these tops, they would also go up Fairfield and Seat Sandal – and 30 more besides, all within 24hrs. The challenge is named after a Keswick hotelier who first completed the route in 1932, to mark his 42nd birthday. The record for the fastest time is held by Billy Bland who completed it in 13hrs and 53mins in 1982.

The path gets steeper and rockier as it follows **Raise Beck** downstream – all the way to **Dunmail Raise** via a series of delightful waterfalls. As the gill opens out, bear left along a narrow trail through the bracken. Keep left at a fork. The path becomes indistinct as it nears a ladder stile beside the road. Continue walking parallel with the fence on your right and then cross it via a stile above the parking area at Dunmail Raise.

WALKS FROM
BORROWDALE AND
BUTTERMERE

Kirk Fell and, behind that, Pillar from Windy Gap (Walk 9)

Walk 7

Scafell Pike

At 978m, Scafell Pike is England's highest mountain and, as such, commands some of the most magnificent views in the Lake District. It's highly unlikely you'll have the summit to yourself, but don't let the mountain's immense popularity overshadow what is, without a doubt, one of the best days out in the entire National Park. Starting from Seathwaite in Borrowdale, we take one of the classic routes – up to Esk Hause via Grains Gill. A broad, rocky ridge – one of the finest miles in Lakeland – is then followed to the roof of England. The return is via the Corridor Route, dropping to Styhead Tarn through some of the grandest mountain scenery this side of the Scottish border. Truly a walk of superlatives!

Scafell Pike from Great End

Start/finish	Seathwaite in Borrowdale (NY 235 123). The roadside parking leading to Seathwaite fills up early, so walkers may need to park in the National Trust pay-and-display car park in Seatoller (NY 245 138), 1.9km from the start of the walk.
Distance	14.5km (9 miles)
Total ascent	1035m (3400ft)
Grade	4
Walking time	6hrs
Terrain	Clear valley paths; broad, stony ridge
Maps	OS Explorers OL4 and OL6; or OS Landrangers 89 or 90
Refreshments	Yew Tree Country Restaurant, Seatoller
Transport	Buses 78 and, summer only, 77/77A serve Seatoller

Having parked on the road leading to Seathwaite, walk south and follow the track into the farmyard and out the other end – signposted Styhead and Esk Hause. After crossing the hump-back **Stockley Bridge** and going through a gate in a wall, turn left immediately.

Grains Gill

A clear path follows **Grains Gill** upstream, eventually crossing back to the other side via a narrow bridge. The path becomes considerably rougher and steeper as the gill narrows and deepens.

It's a tough slog towards the end, but eventually, with Great End's mighty northern buttresses looming above, the path crosses the gill and then swings left to continue climbing at a more sedate angle. Bear right at an obvious fork. One more short climb brings you to **Esk Hause** to be greeted by an amazing panorama of mountains ringing Eskdale. Turn right at the path junction here. Wilder, more rugged country awaits...

The path quickly climbs out of Calf Cove and up to a fairly flat, grassy area.

For a short detour on to **Great End** (910m), turn right along a faint path at the top of this climb. As the path peters out among the rocks, swing left on grass to join a clearer path along which you turn right to make your way on to the broad summit. There is little difference in height between the two cairns, both perched on rock piles. The one to the right is marked on Ordnance Survey maps as the highest point, but there is a slightly better view to be had from the one on the left, reached by following a line of cairns.

Having visited the top, follow cairns back across the summit and down the path. This soon cuts across the grassy area above Calf Cove to rejoin the main ridge route, along which you turn right.

The path now climbs through an area of boulders and continues past **Ill Crag**, the rocky summit of which is over to the left. After the next dip in the path, climb the side of **Broad Crag** and descend once more before starting the final, tiring ascent to the summit of Scafell Pike. The highest war memorial in the country is located on the summit cairn on Scafell Pike (see Walk 9).

Looking down on the Corridor Route with Great End on the right and Styhead Tarn, centre left

Needless to say, there are magnificent views to be had from the top, and, on a clear day, the **Isle of Man** can be seen. The fells visible are too many to mention, but Great Gable is one that stands out from the rest, as is Scafell, the Pike's little brother to the south-west, guarded by the formidable rock-face of Broad Stand.

From the summit, take the cairned path north-west. In 100m, bear right at a fork. As you reach a particularly large cairn at the edge of the main summit area, your descent begins. It isn't especially steep, but it's all on loose stones and boulders, so can be tiresome.

Nearing the grassy area at the base of Lingmell – and just before the path swings left – take the narrower path on your right. It's hard to spot among all the rocks, so you need to watch carefully for it, or else you could end up down in Wasdale.

Having crossed the two arms of the beck feeding into **Piers Gill**, keep straight ahead. You get a dramatic view down this dark, forbidding ravine as you cross the head of it. Ignore the path to the left immediately after the gill.

The **Corridor Route** continues its generally downward trend surrounded by magnificent mountain scenery. Great Gable often seems to dominate, but turn

The dome of rock and scree that is Great Gable

round from time to time to enjoy the view back to Lingmell and, below it, Piers Gill, which creates an amazing slash in the landscape. The path is generally straightforward, although you do encounter a 'bad step' along the way – a short section of bare rock that will require hands.

About 2.6km beyond the summit of Scafell Pike, just after crossing Skew Gill and before the path begins climbing towards **Sty Head**, take a faint path on the left. Don't worry if you miss it – it simply cuts a corner and, whichever route you take, you still have to climb on to the high ground above **Styhead Tarn** and then turn left along a clear path.

When you reach the stretcher box at a crossing of paths, turn right. Continue past the tarn on this clear path and cross the beck at a bridge. The bridleway eventually drops to the valley bottom where it goes through a gate and crosses Stockley Bridge. Swing left to retrace your steps to Seathwaite.

Walk 8

Glaramara and Allen Crags

*There's something inexplicably pleasing about the high ground linking
Glaramara (783m) with Allen Crags (785m). It's hard to pinpoint its charm:
whether it's the near views of dramatic summits such as Great End and Great
Gable, or the feeling of being in the heart of the mountains, surrounded and
dwarfed by grandeur, or simply the ridge itself, constantly undulating and
with pools hidden among rocky basins. This walk approaches Glaramara
from Borrowdale via Thornythwaite Fell, and then returns via Angle Tarn,
Stake Pass and the easy-going path through Langstrath, the 'long valley'.*

The long return route through gorgeous Langstrath

Start/finish	Borrowdale School in Stonethwaite (NY 258 140). The car park, with honesty box, can be used outside of school hours. Otherwise, park on the roadside nearby.
Distance	17.4km (10¾ miles)
Total ascent	955m (3140ft)
Grade	3/4
Walking time	6¼hrs
Terrain	Mostly clear fell paths; easy scramble can be avoided; boggy, pathless stretches; long valley return
Maps	OS Explorers OL4 and OL6; or OS Landrangers 89 or 90
Refreshments	Langstrath Inn, Stonethwaite
Transport	Buses 78 and, summer only, 77/77A stop nearby

From the school car park, turn left along the road and then take the lane on the left – signposted Borrowdale Road via Chapel Farm. Cut diagonally across the farmyard to pass to the right of the whitewashed building. In about 150m, turn right – signposted Burthwaite Bridge.

Turn left at the road and then left along the **Thorneythwaite Farm** track – signposted Seathwaite. About 80m after leaving the road, go through a farm gate on the left.

Borrowdale and, in the distance, Skiddaw, from Thornythwaite Fell

A faint trail climbs beside the wall before joining a clearer route from the right. This passes through patchy woodland and a fenced area grazed by cattle before reaching a gate that gives access to the open fell.

A reasonably well-trodden path heads steadily up on to **Thornythwaite Fell**. There are one or two rocky sections to negotiate as well as some boggy patches where you need to be particularly careful not to lose sight of the route. The path splits on a few occasions, but these strands are always reunited. The general direction, once you're finally on Thornythwaite Fell, is south.

There's plenty of interest in the landscape as the path gains height.

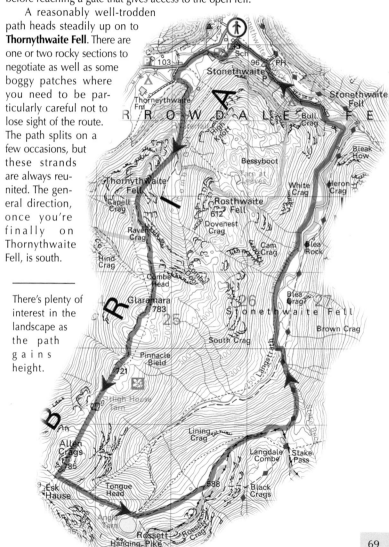

Looking back down into Borrowdale on the early part of the ascent

Across the valley to the east are the many crags of **Rosthwaite Fell**, culminating, at the lonely head of Combe Gill, in the buttress of Combe Head. Looking further afield, Skiddaw, Blencathra and Helvellyn are visible to the north and east, while the western vista is dominated by Great Gable, Lingmell and Great End. The top of Scafell Pike also briefly puts in an appearance.

As you near the rock face protecting the summit of **Glaramara**, you'll see the cairn marking the top of Combe Head about 300 metres to the east. Soon after this, the path forks. Follow the clearest route right – over stepping stones and up to the base of the scramble on to Glaramara. As you reach the rocks, the way ahead may not seem obvious. The conventional route goes straight up the steep rockface. Walking poles need to be stashed away safely, because you'll need your hands for this bit. Safe ledges, where you can rest and decide on your next move, divide the six-metre climb into easily manageable sections.

The worst is over within the first few manoeuvres, but if you can't face it, there is an **easier alternative**. Simply swing right at the base of the scramble, skirting the base of the rocks. You soon pick up a faint path that swings left through an easy gap in the fell's defences. To then reach the summit cairn, bear left at the top.

Most of the major fell groupings are visible from the summit, including the Langdales and the Coniston fells. On a clear day, the Forest of Bowland can also be seen in the distance.

The next target is Allen Crags to the south-west, but the way ahead is unclear at first. Head south from the summit and then pass to the right of a small pool. Pass to the left of a second cairn-topped summit and then join the path coming down from it – descending over boulders. To say the way ahead – clearer now – is undulating is something of an understatement. First, the path drops; then it goes up; then, with the magnificent north face of Great End straight ahead, it descends; then it climbs again…And so it goes on, all the way to **Allen Crags** – across rocky terrain.

The top of **Allen Crags** is marked by a cairn. It's a fantastic spot: you look straight across the vast expanse of Esk Hause to the Irish Sea. Paths come and go in all directions on the pass, promising many adventures on the high fells.

Rossett Pike, right, and the Langdale Pikes seen from near Allen Crags

Descend from Allen Crags on a stony path – towards the shelter below **Esk Hause**. Just before reaching it, turn left, soon joining a clear path descending south-east. You will soon see **Angle Tarn** below, sitting darkly at the foot of Bow Fell.

Immediately after crossing the tarn's outlet stream, turn left. Ignore the steps up to the right as you follow a mostly level path across dull, grassy terrain. Regrettably, you've now literally turned your back on the drama of the high central fells. The path becomes indistinct across a boggy area; keep heading north-east and you'll soon pick it up again.

As the ground on your right drops away, you can see Pike o' Stickle on the other side of Langdale Combe. Keep to the clear path along the edge of the high ground here, soon enjoying views down Langstrath. The path drops slightly. About 2km beyond Angle Tarn, as the path begins swinging right, strike off left (north-east).

As you begin descending, swing east, up and over a small, grassy spur, to drop on to the Stake Pass path. Turn left here to descend tight zig-zags, following **Stake Beck** as it crashes down through a series of noisy waterfalls. Nearing the valley bottom, cross the bridge over the beck. Follow the path on the other side for about 20m and then strike off left (north north-west) over damp, pathless ground to reach the bridge over **Langstrath Beck**.

Having crossed, turn right. The path is reasonably clear as you make your way downstream. About 1.1km after crossing Langstrath Beck, the path all but disappears on reaching a flat, grassy area. The wall directly ahead is crossed via a gate next to a large boulder close to the beck.

Once through the gate, you're on a clear track that leads all the way back to Stonethwaite. It makes a decisive swing left on reaching a particularly noisy section of beck. The wide track eventually becomes a surfaced lane and drops into the hamlet, passing the Langstrath Country Inn on its way back to the school car park.

Walk 9

Great Gable (from Honister)

Great Gable is one of the most recognisable, and iconic, of Lakeland peaks: a massive dome of rock standing isolated from its neighbours and rearing up steeply on all sides. The views from the top are truly awesome, taking in the magnificent Scafell range as well as Wast Water, directly below, and the Irish Sea coast. There's no easy way on to its 899m summit, girdled by a mess of crags, pinnacles and shattered rock, but starting the walk from Honister Pass involves less ascent than other routes. It approaches the mountain using Moses' Trod and then ascends from the north-east. The return route crosses Green Gable (801m), Brandreth (715m) and Grey Knotts (697m).

The impressive view of Ennerdale from Windy Gap

Start/finish	National Trust pay-and-display car park at Honister Pass (NY 225 135)
Distance	8.9km (5½ miles)
Total ascent	715m (2350ft)
Grade	2/3
Walking time	4¼hrs
Terrain	Stony fell tracks; steep, loose ascents and descents; open, grassy fell
Maps	OS Explorer OL4; or OS Landrangers 89 or 90
Refreshments	Café at Honister Slate Mine
Transport	Summer only, bus 77/77A

Walk to the western end of the car park, climb the steps beside the youth hostel and then go left. Turn left to enter the **Honister Slate Mine** site. From the visitor centre, cross to the southern side of the car park and take the clear track heading uphill. After about 100m, turn left at a mountain rescue collection cairn to begin climbing a stony path.

As wooden sleepers higher up the path suggest, you're following the line of an old quarry tramway. It ascends steadily for about 700m and then reaches a raised section, named on Ordnance Survey 1:25,000 maps as the Drum House. This building, of which only the foundations remain, housed the tram's winding gear. Turn sharp left at the Drum House to follow a clear, cairned route gently ascending along the western flanks of Grey Knotts. Haystacks, High Stile and Pillar are clearly visible to the right, and, before long, Buttermere and Crummock Water also put in an appearance.

About 500m beyond the Drum House, the path forks. Keep left, along the higher, clearer path.

Buttermere, with Crummock Water behind, from Moses' Trod

After passing a redundant metal fencepost, you'll see a wire fence immediately ahead. The main path veers left here, but you need to keep straight ahead to cross the fence via a stile. There's not much of a path beyond the fence, but, if you head south-west for a few metres, the way ahead soon becomes more obvious. Known as **Moses' Trod**, it swings left and then curves round the western slopes of Green Gable.

Moses' Trod is an old **packhorse route** that was once used to move slate from Honister to Wasdale for transportation on to the port of Ravenglass. It was named after Moses Rigg, a quarryman who, legend has it, illegally made whisky from bog water and then smuggled it across the fells to Wasdale with his pony-loads of slate.

Great Gable is an imposing mountain from whichever angle you look at it. As you approach via Moses' Trod, it is the north face which looks down on you – a huge mass of grey buttresses and scree fans. Its nearest neighbour to the west, looming on the other side of the valley, is Kirk Fell.

About 1.5km after crossing the fence, you'll find yourself standing at the foot of Gable's steep slopes. There's a large cairn to the left of the path here. Immediately after this, turn left along a faint trail to begin the tortuous climb to

Windy Gap. The path is grassy at first, but becomes loose and stony after passing through an area of boulders. It's little more than scree in its higher stages.

A magnificent mountain scene greets you from the large cairn in **Windy Gap**. Great End with its tremendous gullies looks particularly impressive to the south-east, but don't forget to turn round and look back. The pleasing symmetry of Ennerdale's slopes inevitably draws the eye; tall, upright Pillar looms sentinel-like over what remains of the valley's dark plantations.

From the cairn, turn right (south-west) to climb **Great Gable**. A narrow path first edges around the south-east side of Gable Crag. As the route veers right, you face a steep incline criss-crossed by loose rock and gritty paths. It's hard to decide which way to go. The loose path weaving its way up to the right is extremely unstable in places. Keep left for a slightly more solid, albeit rockier route to the top.

Dale Head is seen on the descent to Honister Pass at the end of the walk

Reaching **Gable's summit**, your efforts are rewarded by fantastic views in all directions and a wonderful sense of satisfaction. No other mountain of its stature in the Lake District stands so far removed from its neighbours: and it's this isolation, this feeling of 'airiness', that gives this great dome of rock its uniqueness. The Scafell range seems to be just a stone's throw away – with the great, dark gash of Piers Gill clearly visible from this angle. Also putting in an appearance for the first time is Wast Water to the south-west. For even better views, particularly of Wasdale far below, head over to the Westmorland Cairn. Details of how to find this ancient pile of rocks perched on the edge of the mountain's summit area are provided in Walk 13.

When you can tear yourself away from the top, retrace your steps to Windy Gap. It is easy to get disorientated on Gable's rock-strewn, featureless summit, so make sure you don't follow the wrong line of cairns down the mountain. Head north-east at first to pick up a reasonably clear line down.

Cross Windy Gap and continue up the other side – on to the summit of **Green Gable**, graced by two shelters. From here, the views to the north open out, taking in Skiddaw and Blencathra.

A clear, cairned path drops away from the summit (north-east). About 250m after leaving the top – as you approach a rocky mound – bear left at an indistinct fork. (There is a temptation to drift right with the clearer path, but this would take you down into Sourmilk Gill.) Heading roughly north, the route follows a line of rusty old fenceposts. It drops to the right of a group of small tarns in a grassy saddle. From here, continue north, climbing mostly pathless fellside on to **Brandreth**. Don't be tempted by the cairned path that initially heads north from the tarns – it quickly swings north-west.

The top of Brandreth, just 400m up from the tarns, is marked by a pile of stones with several old fenceposts sticking out of it. From here, follow a faint path north north-east towards another fencepost and then down to a fence corner.

Don't go through the gate; instead, walk with the fence on your left towards **Grey Knotts** (north north-east), passing a couple of small tarns along the way. Soon after the fence bends sharp right, cross a stile in it. But keep faith with it, soon following it round to the left and then crossing the next stile.

Turn left. The path is a lot clearer now as it makes its way down to Honister Pass, still following the fence. Your eyes will undoubtedly be firmly on the ground as you pick your way down the rockier sections of path, but take some time to pause and look across the pass to the impressive crags and disused slate workings on Dale Head.

Finally, the path drops to a stile in a fence. Once over this, cross the slate mine's yard, making for the gate below the youth hostel. Go through this to re-enter the car park where the walk started.

MOUNTAINS OF REMEMBRANCE

Just after World War One, the Fell and Rock Climbing Club purchased a huge tract of land taking in Great Gable, Kirk Fell, Grey Knotts, Allen Crags, Glaramara, Great End, Broad Crags, Lingmell, Green Gable, Brandreth, Base Brown and Seathwaite Fell as a memorial to members who had died during the conflict. These mountains were then gifted to the National Trust to hold for the nation. A plaque, bearing a relief map of the area and the names of the fallen, can be found on the north side of the summit rocks. The plaque was first unveiled in June 1924.

Since then, whatever the weather – and it can get pretty bad in November – hundreds of walkers and climbers make their way every Remembrance Sunday to the top of this famous fell to remember those who died while serving their country.

But Great Gable wasn't the first fell to be dedicated in this manner. In 1919, the summit of Scafell Pike and 16 hectares surrounding it were donated to the National Trust by Lord Leconfield in memory of the local men who had died in World War One. An inscription on the summit cairn, the highest war memorial in the country, commemorates the men who 'fell for God and King, for freedom, peace and right in the Great War 1914–18'. And, in Borrowdale, Sir William Hamer gave Castle Crag to the National Trust in memory of his son and men from the valley killed in the same conflict.

Walk 10

Hay Stacks

It may not be the mightiest of Lake District mountains, but Hay Stacks (597m) has a special quality that makes it a favourite among fell-walkers. Dwarfed by its neighbours, it provides inspiring views across Ennerdale to Pillar, Kirk Fell and Great Gable as well as some breathtaking glimpses of the Buttermere valley. This walk uses a conventional – albeit rough and rocky – route to the summit, but then descends a less well-trodden path: a quiet and more interesting alternative to the badly eroded bridleway on the northern side of Warnscale Beck.

Pillar from Hay Stacks

Start/finish	Gatesgarth Farm, 3km SE of Buttermere village (NY 194 150)
Distance	6.9km (4¼ miles)
Total ascent	540m (1770ft)
Grade	1
Walking time	3hrs
Terrain	Mostly open fell with steep, rocky ascent
Maps	OS Explorer OL4; or OS Landrangers 89 or 90
Refreshments	Pubs and cafés in nearby Buttermere
Transport	Summer only, bus 77/77A

From the car park opposite Gatesgarth Farm, cross the road and go through the walkers' gate. Just after crossing a wooden bridge, known as **Peggy's Bridge**, go through the gate and head steeply uphill to the right of a small group of trees. When you reach the top of this wooded area, bear left with the fence and continue uphill.

As you ascend, don't be tempted to stay on the right-hand side of the wall that comes snaking steeply up from the valley below; you need to go through a gap soon after first encountering it. The path gets steeper and rougher as you toil uphill to **Scarth Gap**.

Turning left at a large cairn in the pass, hands are needed for the rocky ascent of the western ridge of **Hay Stacks**.

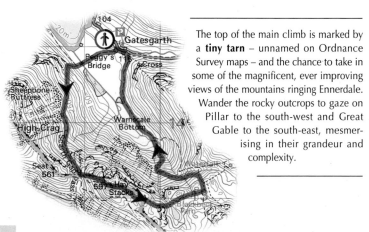

The top of the main climb is marked by a **tiny tarn** – unnamed on Ordnance Survey maps – and the chance to take in some of the magnificent, ever improving views of the mountains ringing Ennerdale. Wander the rocky outcrops to gaze on Pillar to the south-west and Great Gable to the south-east, mesmerising in their grandeur and complexity.

On Hay Stacks

When you can drag yourself away from this spell-binding scene, locate the path along the northern edge of the fell and follow it to Innominate Tarn, sitting serenely in a depression between rocky, heathery knolls.

Hay Stacks was guidebook writer **Alfred Wainwright's** favourite Lakeland summit, and it was here, on the shores of Innominate Tarn, that his ashes were scattered after his death in 1991.

Passing to the left of the tarn, the path soon swings left to drop slightly and pass beneath a dark crag before crossing the outlet stream of **Blackbeck Tarn**. Looking down the gully on the left here, there is a jaw-dropping view to the green valley below, including Buttermere and Crummock Water. Beyond the outlet stream, the path climbs again and passes around the side of Green Crag. It is soon joined by another path and then crosses some damp ground. Before long, you will see a less well-used path to the right, heading off at a right angle to the main track. Our route swings left here, aiming, it seems, directly for the quarry workings on Fleetwith in the distance. When the track then swings right again,

Buttermere and, behind that, Crummock Water seen from Hay Stacks

leave it by turning left along a narrower path to begin the descent. This path, the start of which is easy to miss, winds its way steadily to **Warnscale Bottom**, passing close to Warnscale Bothy along the way and cutting beneath Hay Stacks' dark, northern cliffs.

Cross the bridge over Warnscale Beck and follow the faint path up to a clear bridleway, along which you bear left. Turn left at the road to return to the car park at Gatesgarth Farm.

Walk 11
Grasmoor and Gasgale Crags

This relatively short, but surprisingly tough walk involves a steep, stony ascent and an even steeper and stonier descent. But it's those difficult sections that make all the good bits that much more enjoyable and leave you with an immense sense of satisfaction. The route climbs Grasmoor (852m) via the Lad Hows ridge with its superb views of beautiful Crummock Water. After enjoying a fine stroll along the top of Dove Crags, it drops to Coledale Hause before climbing Hopegill Head (770m). A wonderfully airy ridge path then leads along the top of Gasgale Crags before the descent from Whiteside.

The top of Gasgale Crags

Start/finish	Small parking area at the bottom of Cinderdale Beck on the eastern side of Crummock Water, 3km from Buttermere village (NY 162 192). There are two parking areas about 150m apart here. The walk description starts from the one further S.
Distance	10.3km (6½ miles)
Total ascent	995m (3270ft)
Grade	3/4
Walking time	4½hrs
Terrain	Open fell; steep, stony ascent and descent; rocky ridge
Maps	OS Explorer OL4; or OS Landranger 89
Refreshments	The Barn teashop at New House Farm near Lorton; Croft House Café, Bridge Hotel and Buttermere Court Hotel, all in Buttermere village; Kirkstile Inn in Loweswater
Transport	Summer only, bus 77/77A

From the parking area, cross **Cinderdale Beck** and head upstream – signposted Grasmoor. The path isn't obvious at first, but you soon pick up a trail through the bracken. Keep close to the beck until, after about 400m, it swings away to the left. Later, you will get one more glimpse of the beck far below before the path swings right on to Lad Hows. The spectacular views now are dominated by Red Pike and High Stile to the south, with Rannerdale Knotts in the middle ground, a small but defiant fell standing guard over Crummock Water.

The bracken is soon replaced by heather and bilberry as the path swings left along the top of the ridge. The gradient eases for a while as you enjoy the views to the

The early part of the ascent provides a good view back towards Rannerdale Knotts, the High Stile ridge and Crummock Water

right, across Rannerdale Beck towards Whiteless Pike and Wandope. The ascent is steep in places, and becomes more so the higher you climb. The last part is the toughest and calls for an extra hard push as boots fight for a firm purchase on the loose stones.

With a sigh of relief, you'll feel the gradient ease and the ground underfoot turn to springy turf as you make your way on to the grassy summit. Here, you meet a clearer path, along which you turn left to reach the shelter at the top of **Grasmoor**.

The outlook from the flat, grassy summit of **Grasmoor** is truly spectacular – and far-reaching. To the south, the Scafell group is an impressive sight. On a clear day, you'll be able to see Snaefell on the Isle of Man and Cross Fell in the Pennines – two summits that are 135km apart. To the north are Hopegill Head and the rather impressive Gasgale Crags, which form part of your return route.

Leaving the well-walked path on the southern side of Grasmoor, pick up a trail along the northern edge of the fell. Walk east north-east from the shelter, almost parallel with the path you followed up to the summit furniture, which you'll be able to see over to the right at first. After 100m or so, you'll find a trail along the edge of the high ground. Whenever it forks, bear left, keeping to the rim of the fell and enjoying some great views down on to Dove Crags and across to Gasgale Crags.

As you draw level with Eel Crag, the descent briefly steepens. On nearing the top end of Liza Beck, the path practically disappears. Step across the beck and take a few more strides

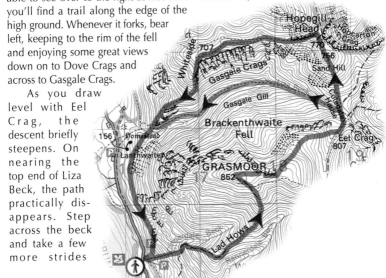

Approaching the top of Whiteside

east north-east to reach a clear path. Turn left along this and immediately you'll encounter a prominent cairn. Bear left here and, in a short while, keep right at a fork. You quickly encounter another clear path in **Coledale Hause**, along which you turn left. Reaching a junction of paths at the base of the slope, keep straight ahead (north). To cut short the walk, having turned left at the prominent cairn, keep straight on to follow Liza Beck downstream. You then pick up the walk description at the bridge below Whin Ben.

What is at first a pleasant, grassy path on to **Sand Hill** soon becomes a loose, stony mess as it climbs more steeply, but this a doddle after the Lad Hows climb.

The path splits on occasions on the way up – take any route. From the top of Sand Hill, the path drops slightly and then climbs to the top of **Hopegill Head**.

The summit is marked by a **tiny cairn** perched on a small rocky outcrop. It's a great place to sit and enjoy the views north, into Scotland, as you tuck into your sandwiches.

From the summit, head west, following the clear path along the top of the ridge linking Hopegill Head with Whiteside. The ground to the left drops away steeply on to **Gasgale Crags**, but the slope on the right is slightly gentler, so if unnerved by the slight sense of exposure, keep right on encountering rocky sections.

From the top of **Whiteside** at the western end of the ridge, the path briefly becomes a little indistinct: keep close to the southern edge of the fell and you'll soon pick up a loose, stony path heading downhill. The first tricky section starts about 300m from the top. It calls for surefootedness as you carefully pick your way down through the fractured rock and loose stones. The second one, involving bare rock that becomes slippery in wet weather, can be easily avoided by taking a trail to the right through the heather. There is then one more steep section as you come over the top of Whin Ben and plummet down the other side, but after that... well, you're practically back in the valley now.

Nearing **Liza Beck**, keep left at two faint forks to reach a clear track just above a bridge. After crossing the bridge, head south-west up the short embankment immediately in front of you. At the top, keep straight on, ignoring wider paths to the left and right. The narrow trail through the bracken soon swings south, hugging the base of the fell. It's now about 1.5km back to the parking area where the walk started, but, as long as you aren't tempted by any other paths heading uphill to the left, the going should be easy all the way.

As you reach Cinderdale Common, resist a path to the right that drops to the first of the two car parks. Continue for a further 120m and then, on nearing Cinderdale Beck, you'll see a path heading up to the left. Turn right here and then swing left to drop back into the parking area where the walk started.

WALKS FROM THE
WESTERN VALLEYS

On the ridge leading to High Crag (Walk 12)

Walk 12

The High Stile ridge

Starting from the western edge of the National Park, this magnificent ridge walk grows in grandeur as you make your way along it. It takes in Great Borne (616m), Starling Dodd (633m), Red Pike (755m), High Stile (807m) and High Crag (744m), a line of fells that becomes progressively craggier as you gain height. Every step takes you closer to the heart of the Lake District as the surrounding mountains, including some of the highest in England, gradually close in around you.

Red Pike from High Stile

Start/finish	Bowness Knott car park on N side of Ennerdale Water (NY 109 153)
Distance	20.3km (12½ miles)
Total ascent	1130m (3700ft)
Grade	4
Walking time	7½hrs
Terrain	Open fell; indistinct paths at times; steep, rocky descent; valley track
Maps	OS Explorer OL4; or OS Landranger 89
Refreshments	Fox and Hounds and the Shepherds Arms Hotel in nearby Ennerdale Bridge
Transport	None

Leave the car park and turn right along the road. About 300m after a cattle grid, climb a stile in the fence on your right – next to Rake Beck. This stream acts as your guide almost all the way to the top of Great Borne. A path heads steeply up the grassy hillside, just to the left of the remains of an old sheepfold. You soon cross a gill at the base of the low-lying crags of **Brown How**. The climb then temporarily eases as you reach a fork next to a large boulder. Turn left here to climb the heather-covered slope. Part way up, you pass an unusual round drystone structure.

This structure is a **goose bield**, sometimes referred to as a fox bield. A dead goose would have been hung on a pole over the top of the trap. An apron of stones around the outside of the structure made it easy for the fox to gain entry to the enclosure, but once inside, the smooth, high walls of the interior made escape impossible.

Looking out across High Stile's steep northern ridge with Dale Head behind and the Helvellyn range in the background

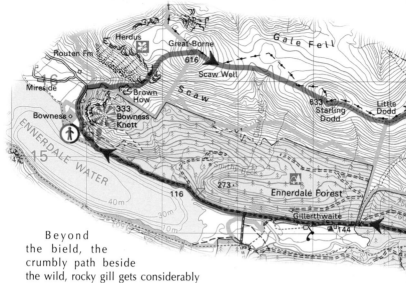

Beyond the bield, the crumbly path beside the wild, rocky gill gets considerably steeper, and you will encounter one short section of bare rock where you may need to use your hands.

Eventually, the lung-bursting part of the ascent comes to an end and you say goodbye to Rake Beck. The climb, however, is not yet over; a clear path swings right and picks its way up between piles of boulders and small outcrops of granite.

On reaching the trig pillar and shelter on **Great Borne**, you are suddenly met with a dramatic scene: a semi-circle of mountains from Whiteside and Grasmoor in the north-east to Crag Fell and Haycock in the south, taking in Robinson, Dale Head, Helvellyn, Great Gable and Pillar on the way round.

From the trig pillar and shelter on Great Borne, drop to the fence north-east of the summit, where you will find a grassy path. Turn right along this, following the fence downhill. The path keeps close to the fence after it kinks left at **Scaw Well**, but then the route swings right, making more directly for Starling Dodd. You briefly encounter another fence on your way across, but part company with it before the climb proper begins. With legs still tired from the Rake Beck climb, the walk up **Starling Dodd** can be a plod, but it is short-lived and you are soon standing beside the jumble of fence posts piled up on the summit.

The faint, grassy path continues down the hill's eastern flank and makes its way towards Red Pike, about 2.1km away. You will encounter a line of rusty old fenceposts as you begin climbing. These act as your guide now – all the way along the ridge and down to Scarth Gap. They bypass the true summit of **Red Pike**, but the top is just a few metres up to the left, if you feel the need to 'bag' it.

As you crest a rise and see High Stile ahead, the nature of the walk suddenly changes. Follow the rough path along the northern edge of the fell. The grassy, heathery moorland is behind you now; ahead, the dominant feature is rock. Great rock chutes plunge valleyward from beneath the imposing buttresses of High Stile, the highest point on the route. The path becomes rocky underfoot as you make your way uphill again, always keeping an eye on those fenceposts to ensure you're not straying off route. The cairn at the top of the climb isn't the highest point on **High Stile**, but it is the more impressive viewpoint, so this walk misses out the true summit, which lies on a spur to the north-east.

Continue following the fenceposts south-east across the mostly flat summit area and then swing right. Ahead and just below now is the enjoyable, but all-too-short ridge leading on to **High Crag**. You lose a little height before swinging left again along this narrower section of the route.

The high-level fun comes to an end on the summit of High Crag; now, the descent begins. The steep path down Gamlin End is horribly loose at first, and you lose a lot of height over a short distance. Cruelly, once this descent is over, there is still one small hill to climb before you drop to the valley. This is **Seat** and

Looking back on the final pull up to Great Borne.
Ennerdale Water can be seen below

the ridge path continues up and over it, again following the fenceposts. It is only 561m high, but the short drop into Scarth Gap is a killer at this point in the day.

When you reach **Scarth Gap** – the pass between the High Stile range and Hay Stacks – turn right. The path isn't always clear as it crosses a boggy area, but there are cairns to guide you. It keeps close to the high ground on your right at first and becomes more obvious as it crosses a beck on your left.

Eventually, you drop on to a wide track in **Ennerdale**. Turn right, through a gate, and try not to be too disheartened by the sign indicating that it's another six miles back to the car park. It is a long walk, but Ennerdale is a magical place to be at the end of the day.

WILD ENNERDALE

The Wild Ennerdale project was set up in 2002 as an attempt by the three major landowners – the Forestry Commission, National Trust and United Utilities – to allow nature a greater say in the valley's future. The appearance of this loneliest of Lakeland valleys is already changing.

Sitka spruces, planted in Ennerdale in the 20th century, are being felled and, as a result, native broadleaf species such as oak, birch, rowan and willow are returning. Spruce is allowed to regrow for the sake of diversity, but it is removed if it starts dominating. No conifers have been planted since 2002, except juniper, which is thought to have once flourished here. The name of the dale itself, long thought to be connected to the name of a chieftain, Anund, might even come from the old Norse word for juniper, einir.

Semi-wild Galloway cattle roam freely. They were introduced in 2006 when ecologists advised the Wild Ennerdale team that the grazing and disturbance caused by large herbivores, largely absent from British forests, was necessary to open the way for different plant species. Like everything else in the valley, they are mostly left to their own devices.

There are other mammals in Ennerdale too: red squirrels are most often seen in the western woodland; otters have recolonised the valley; both red and roe deer frequent the area; and there have even been unconfirmed sightings of the elusive pine marten.

After about 5.3km, you pass the youth hostel at **High Gillerthwaite**, soon after which you should ignore a track to the left. The next major landmark is the eastern end of **Ennerdale Water**. As you draw level with that, it's only about 1.9km back to the car park.

Walk 13

Great Gable (from Wasdale Head)

After climbing Great Gable (899m) from Honister Pass in walk nine, this route tackles it from Wasdale Head, a considerably tougher ascent amid even more dramatic scenery. Using the continuation of Moses' Trod, it first heads up Gavel Neese before swinging on to Beck Head and then clambering up the mountain's north-west ridge. The descent is via the Breast Route, Gable's 'gentlest' face – but don't go expecting an easy stroll; it's still very steep. From Sty Head, as most walkers head off down the well-walked path along the base of Gable's southern slopes, the walk picks up the old Pony Route. Dwarfed by the majesty of the Scafell range above, this little used, mostly grassy route eases its way down to the valley bottom, fording several gills along the way.

Wasdale from the stony Beck Head path

Start/finish	Wasdale Head village green (NY 186 084)
Distance	9.3km (5¾ miles)
Total ascent	850m (2790ft)
Grade	3/4
Walking time	5hrs
Terrain	Valley track; steep ascent and descent; rough, rocky ground on fell; return on grass with fords to cross
Maps	OS Explorer OL6; or OS Landranger 89
Refreshments	Wasdale Head Inn
Transport	None

Take the bridleway on the eastern side of the village green – signposted Sty Head Pass. It starts just to the left of Lingmell House bed and breakfast and soon passes tiny St Olaf's Church. With the mesmerising image of Great Gable's scree and crag-covered face straight ahead, the track makes its way up between drystone walls as far as the farm at **Burnthwaite**. On entering the farmyard, bear left, between two stone barns. Go through a gate and turn right along a rough track, continuing up into the valley.

Immediately after crossing the wooden footbridge over Gable Beck, bear left to join a pitched path climbing through the bracken. With Kirk Fell's impressive Ill Gill straight ahead, the path passes through a gate and swings right to gain the south-west shoulder of Great Gable, known as Gavel Neese. It's a steep climb, but all on grass at this stage. Directly ahead, the craggy outline of the Napes adds to the increasingly spec-

tacular scene. Reaching the base of much rougher ground, the pitching ends, the grass disappears and the path swings left to cut across the fellside. The gradient is fractionally easier now, but you won't be aware of that as you struggle upwards, sometimes fighting

The Westmorland Cairn on Great Gable

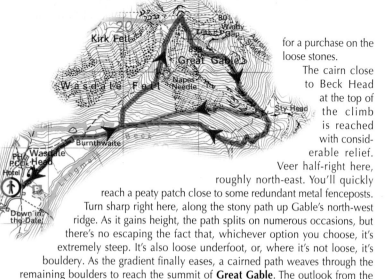

for a purchase on the loose stones.

The cairn close to Beck Head at the top of the climb is reached with considerable relief. Veer half-right here, roughly north-east. You'll quickly reach a peaty patch close to some redundant metal fenceposts. Turn sharp right here, along the stony path up Gable's north-west ridge. As it gains height, the path splits on numerous occasions, but there's no escaping the fact that, whichever option you choose, it's extremely steep. It's also loose underfoot, or, where it's not loose, it's bouldery. As the gradient finally eases, a cairned path weaves through the remaining boulders to reach the summit of **Great Gable**. The outlook from the top, briefly described in Walk 9, is simply amazing. For even better views, head about 150m south-west from the summit rocks.

Perched on the edge of precipitous ground above the Napes is the **Westmorland Cairn**. This 140-year-old pile of moss and lichen-covered stones commands an impressive spot on the mountain. As well as gazing down on Wast Water and across to the Scafells, visitors to its precarious spot can look down on Tophet Bastion and the upper ramparts of the Napes. Rocky ledges nearby provide a great lunch spot away from the summit crowds, few of whom will stray this far from the main routes on and off the mountain.

When you can finally tear yourself away from the views, return to the summit rocks and take the cairned route descending south-east at first. The summit of Great Gable can be a confusing place, even without the clouds that often dwell here, so use a compass to locate the correct path off the mountain. Known as the Breast Route, it swings about as it descends: one minute you're looking across to Glaramara, the next your eyes are fixed on the Scafells. The mostly pitched path may not always seem ideal, but it's far better than the alternative, which is horrendously loose scree.

Eventually, you'll reach the Mountain Rescue stretcher box at **Sty Head**. In mist, turn right here and follow the well-worn path down Gable's southern slopes.

Although difficult to locate, the quieter and more pleasant descent in clear weather is the old Pony Route. To find it, go right at the stretcher box, but then immediately step to the left – along a faint, grassy trod. This heads south at first, disappears as it crosses damp ground, and then briefly veers south-west to descend a small, rocky gap. The path is more obvious now: mostly on grass, it winds its way down to Spouthead Gill.

Close to the base of the **Scafell group**, there is impressive scenery all around. The ravines, in particular, demand attention: Great End's Skew Gill to the south-east and the almost impenetrable Piers Gill to the south-west.

Ill Gill on Kirk Fell

Styhead Tarn

The path fades away on the damp ground close to the beck. Carefully ford the gill to pick up a clearer route on the other side, heading downstream. Following an easy line, it later fords a smaller beck before heading for the confluence of Spouthead Gill and Piers Gill. Carefully ford the former just above their rocky meeting point.

The path continues downstream beside **Lingmell Beck**, along the rock-strewn valley bottom. Soon after a gate in a wall, keep straight ahead at a crossing of paths among the bracken. The main path from Sty Head then joins from the right. Crossing the footbridge over Gable Beck, it's now simply a case of retracing your steps to the parking area, remembering to bear left to walk between the farm buildings at Burnthwaite.

Walk 14

Pillar and Red Pike

Pillar (892m) and Red Pike (821m) are two of the impressive peaks standing at the head of Mosedale, an offshoot of the Wasdale valley. Always in the shadow of England's highest mountains, the walk taking in these two summits is one you won't forget in a hurry. As well as enjoying spectacular views in all directions, it passes through some stunning mountain scenery dominated by imposing crags, glaciated valleys, scree-ridden coves and the occasional grassy plateau on which to rest and savour this thoroughly enjoyable high-level day.

Kirk Fell and, behind, Great Gable from the early part of the climb on to Pillar

Start/finish	National Trust free car park at Overbeck Bridge (NY 168 068), about 2.9km SW of Wasdale Head
Distance	15.8km (9¾ miles)
Total ascent	1080m (3540ft)
Grade	4
Walking time	6¾hrs
Terrain	Road walking; long ascent on valley track; open fell, often steep and on rough ground
Maps	OS Explorers OL4 and OL6; or OS Landranger 89
Refreshments	Wasdale Head Inn
Transport	None

Red Pike with Scafell and Scafell Pike in the distance

From the car park, turn left along the road and walk to **Wasdale Head**. Take the path around the side of the Wasdale Head Inn, passing the Barn Door Shop on your right and then veer right beside **Mosedale Beck**. Go through the small gate and, ignoring the bridge on the left, follow the beck upstream. Bear left when the path splits about 300m beyond the pub. Continuing upstream, keep to the clear track as it skirts the base of the steep western slopes of Kirk Fell. At first, it's a relatively gentle climb into **Mosedale**. There's plenty of time to enjoy this peaceful and often dramatic valley. The views across the dale – to Yewbarrow and Red Pike – and up towards its fearsome head are particularly enthralling.

Having travelled about 2.5km from the Wasdale Head Inn, the path fords Gatherstone Beck, and the uphill work really begins. **Black Sail Pass** is inevitably greeted with some relief.

The views now include the **fells above Buttermere**, and, looking up Ennerdale, Green Gable can be seen. Kirk Fell, on the immediate right, just hides the summit of Great Gable at this point in the walk.

Turn left at the pass. When you reach the cairn at the base of the first set of crags, the path splits in to three. The one on the right marks the start of the climbers' route to Pillar Rock. Take either of the other two: they both involve easy scrambling. As the gradient eases, you are able to look across the valley to the left to the craggy north-east face of Red Pike. Unfortunately though, the short rest is soon over and the long, uphill trudge restarts as you pick your way up through a rocky landscape, following a line of redundant fenceposts. The

103

formidable northern face of Pillar includes a chaotic jumble of shattered crags, boulders and scree, so take some time to stop occasionally and peer over the edge.

Finally, you reach the summit – a grassy plateau with a trig pillar, shelters… and fantastic views!

From the top of **Pillar** all of the major Lake District peaks can be seen, as can the Pennines, the Scottish hills, the Isle of Man and Morecambe Bay. For a glimpse of Pillar Rock, walk to the small shelter to the north of the trig point and then descend the rough path for a few metres. You'll soon be gazing down on the conspicuous lump.

Continuing the walk, head south-west from the trig pillar, following a line of cairns that quickly leads to a clear path. You'll need to watch your footing on this steep, loose descent, but take some time to look up occasionally and take in the fantastic, gnarly landscape ahead. Windgap Cove, Mirk Cove, Black Comb, Steeple and the eastern face of Red Pike consist of little more than scree and crags. In dire emergencies, an horrendously steep scree path heading left from Wind Gap can be used to drop into Mosedale.

Having dropped into the **Wind Gap** saddle, clamber steeply up a jumble of boulders to a cairn above Black Crag. Beyond is a lovely plateau of close-cropped turf – a welcome relief after recent efforts. Just as the path starts climbing from the saddle between this high, grassy area and Little Scoat Fell, bear left at a fork (south veering south-east). With a spectacular, uninterrupted view across to the Scafell group, this narrow path skirts the top of steep, rough ground dropping away to the left. As it climbs towards the summit of Red Pike, the clearest route comes away from the edge. As it does so, bear left to keep to the exposed rim of the fell – not only does the main path bypass the true summit, it misses out on the best views across the abyss of Mosedale.

The top of **Red Pike** is marked by a small cairn. Still hugging the edge of the precipice, descend the grassy slope ahead and keep to the left of a cairn-topped pile of rocks at the end of the summit area. The path is a little indistinct here, but becomes clearer as you descend more steeply. The drop to **Dore Head** is completed via a series of rocky sections with grassy interludes between.

Dore Head sits in a damp saddle between Red Pike and the steep, northern ridge of Yewbarrow. About 100m after passing to the right of a small, dark pool at Dore Head, bear right (south south-west) along a faint, grassy path. This keeps to the eastern side of **Over Beck**.

Wast Water beckons at the end of the day

Losing height at a barely perceptible rate, you eventually pass through a gate in a wall near the southern end of **Yewbarrow** and then meet another wall. Cross the ladder stile and turn sharp right to descend steeply on grass with **Wast Water** straight ahead. Drawing level with a stile on your right, follow the path left to drop to the car park where the walk started.

Walk 15

Scafell

At 964m above sea level, Scafell is England's second highest mountain and yet, in so many ways, it stands head and shoulders above its 977m neighbour, Scafell Pike. A glance at its dark, northern cliffs from Wasdale and you'd be forgiven for thinking that this monster of a mountain was the bigger of the two. Indeed, before altitude could be measured accurately, Scafell was widely thought to be higher than Scafell Pike. Any approach is a tough one, but the walk from Eskdale, although long, does at least avoid the difficulties associated with attacking the mountain from Wasdale. It involves a long walk in across lonely Eskdale Moor and then a descent via Long Green and Slight Side – enjoying fantastic views across Upper Eskdale all the while.

Scafell seen from the early part of the walk

Start/finish	Pay-and-display car park at Dalegarth Station, near Boot, Eskdale (NY 173 007)
Distance	16.7km (10½ miles)
Total ascent	1015m (3330ft)
Grade	4
Walking time	7hrs
Terrain	Open fell, rocky in places; steep, stony ascent; boggy moorland on return
Maps	OS Explorer OL6; or OS Landranger 89
Refreshments	Brook House Inn and Boot Inn in Boot; Fellbites Café at Dalegarth Station
Transport	Dalegarth Station is served by the Ravenglass and Eskdale Railway. For timetables, visit www.ravenglass-railway.co.uk or phone 01229 717171.

Turn left out of the station car park and then left again when you reach the Brook House Inn. Having passed through **Boot**, cross the humpback bridge over **Whillan Beck**. A short section of cobbles leads up to a gate. Keep right after going through this and, in another 110m, go through the gate on your right (it should have a bridleway marker on it).

Bow Fell from Scafell

After 1.3km of steady climbing, mostly beside the wooded ravine containing Whillan Beck, you break free from the walled enclosures. The western slopes of Scafell, visible beyond the shoulder of Great How, appear ahead. A sometimes grassy, sometimes stony track crosses the moody moorland above Whillan Beck.

You are now following the old **Corpse Road**. Before St Olaf's Church at Wasdale Head was licensed for burials, this bridleway was used to transport coffins across the bleak moorland to St Catherine's in Eskdale.

About 800m beyond the last gate, you'll see an old stone building up to the left. The main track swings left here. As it does so, continue straight on – taking a less well-walked path to the right of the bend. After bearing right at the next fork, the mountains of Wasdale make their presence felt, including Kirk Fell, Pillar and Yewbarrow. Keeping right at yet another fork, the path drops to the edge of **Burnmoor Tarn**, crossing

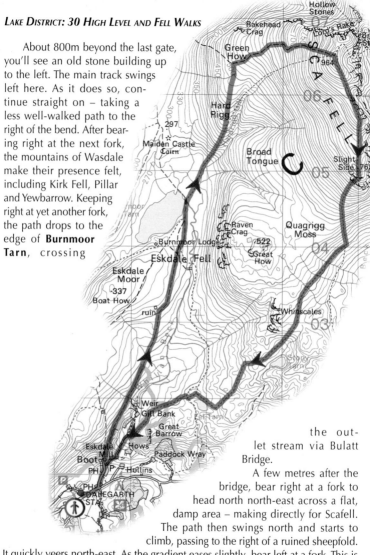

the outlet stream via Bulatt Bridge.

A few metres after the bridge, bear right at a fork to head north north-east across a flat, damp area – making directly for Scafell. The path then swings north and starts to climb, passing to the right of a ruined sheepfold. It quickly veers north-east. As the gradient eases slightly, bear left at a fork. This is slightly more long-winded than the right-hand branch, which cuts a corner, but it provides great views of Wasdale.

The path dawdles across the grassy, western slopes of the mountain, toying with the idea of climbing, but doing very little in the way of gaining altitude. Finally, it makes a decisive swing east north-east, making directly for stonier ground. The path becomes a little less obvious as it steepens, but there are cairns guiding the way. The final pull on to the summit of **Scafell** is through steeply inclined loose rock and stones, providing an arduous finale to an already tiring climb. At the top of the ascent, you are greeted by amazing views to the east – as well as a welcome shelter.

The summit of **England's second highest mountain** is up on the rocks to the right, but you should first wander left to see the crags and gills that make up Scafell's awesome north face. All looks impressive enough until the ground at your feet suddenly drops away, and Scafell reveals just a tiny glimpse of its fearful buttresses and forbidding gullies. This terrifying chasm is Deep Gill. It's an area that rewards exploration, but be careful in misty conditions. Symonds Knott, up to the left, can easily be climbed for a more airy experience.

Having explored the mountain's northern edge, backtrack across the saddle and up to the summit cairn. The view, as you'd expect, is tremendous, taking in

The top of Deep Gill

a wide-ranging panorama. The top of Scafell Pike, seemingly just a stone's throw away across the gulf of Mickledore, is inevitably crawling with people.

PIONEERS OF THE CRAGS

The Lake District is closely associated with the history of rock-climbing and mountaineering. The first recorded ascent of Napes Needle on Great Gable by Walter Parry Haskett Smith, the so-called 'father of British rock-climbing', is regarded as a defining episode in that history: the moment when, in 1886, climbing became a sport.

But more than 80 years before that, Coleridge was writing about his experiences on Scafell: an outing that some regard as the first recorded climb for leisure purposes. He climbed England's second highest mountain in August 1802 from Wasdale via Broad Tongue, a relatively uncomplicated route, but his subsequent descent via Broad Stand was anything but straightforward. He had to ease himself down one tricky rock ledge after another until he realised that, despite being in a very perilous position, he had no choice but to continue descending. Describing the experience later, he wrote: "I had only two more [ledges] to drop down, to return was impossible – but of these two the first was tremendous, it was twice my own height, and the ledge at the bottom was so exceedingly narrow, that if I dropt down upon it I must of necessity have fallen backwards and of course killed myself. My limbs were all in a tremble..."Broad Stand (pictured seen from Scafell Pike) remains an accident blackspot today. Wasdale Mountain Rescue Team records more call-outs to this steep, rocky and often slippery short-cut between Scafell and Scafell Pike than to any other location – and many of the accidents have resulted in death.

From the summit, follow the southern ridge off the mountain, up and over Long Green and then on to **Slight Side**. Keep to the eastern edge as much as possible. There is a slightly less rocky path to the west if you want to avoid the rough ground, but the edge provides the most exciting prospect down into Upper Eskdale and across to the mountains on the other side, including Bow Fell and Crinkle Crags.

The true summit of Slight Side is reached via an easy clamber on sticky rocks, but the main path goes round to the left of it. A faint, cairned trail then drops south, weaving a straightforward route through the rocks before swinging right (west) to descend on grass. Soon after a badly eroded section, the path swings south again.

About 1km beyond the summit of Slight Side, watch carefully for a faint fork, marked by a cairn. Bear right here (south-west). The faint path crosses damp ground with a great sense of remoteness about it. It becomes indistinct when it hits particularly boggy areas, but it can usually be found again, until, that is, it passes close to Cat Cove. If you lose sight of it here, make for the prominent round boulder on a small hillock. From here, you'll see Stony Tarn below. Drop towards the tarn and then pick up a trail about 100m above its north-west shore.

This gradually winds its way down to **Eel Tarn**, all but disappearing into the mire from time to time. If you lose it, the best advice, again, is to head on to high ground to locate Eel Tarn. The general direction is south-west and the path passes

Eel Tarn

Looking out towards Long Green from Scafell

to the north-east of the tarn, keeping some way back from the water's edge, where the ground is swampy.

Having passed Eel Tarn, ignore the path heading left; continue west, across pathless ground and then down beside the outlet stream. You quickly reach a clear track, along which you turn left. Losing height all the while, the track later passes between drystone walls. Watch carefully for a fingerpost down to your right – at a point where the wall kinks right. The track bypasses the signpost, so, if you miss it, you'll miss your turning. Drop to the fingerpost and turn right – through the gate.

Turn left along the track to drop back into Boot. Turn left at the road and then right at the Brook House Inn to return to Dalegarth Station.

WALKS FROM CONISTON
AND LANGDALE

Crinkle Crags from Pike o' Blisco (Walk 18)

Walk 16

The Coniston Fells

Scrambling up rocky mountain spines and striding out along dramatic ridge-tops are among the many highlights of this long, exhilarating hike in the Coniston Fells. Making for a superb day in this neatly compact group of mountains, the route takes in several summits, including Wetherlam (762m), Swirl How (802m), Brim Fell (796m), Coniston Old Man (803m) and Dow Crag (778m). The views are spell-binding throughout and there is lots of detail in the surrounding landscape, both natural and man-made, to sidetrack you. Save this one for a clear day – and allow plenty of time for dawdling and exploring.

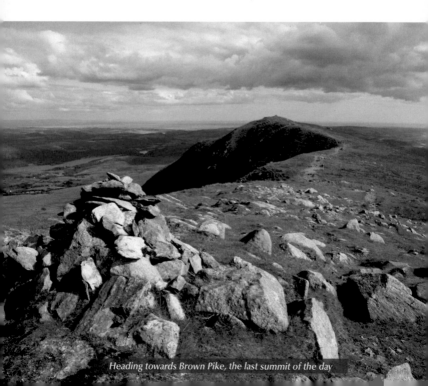

Heading towards Brown Pike, the last summit of the day

Start/finish	Main pay-and-display car park near tourist information centre in Coniston (SD 303 975)
Distance	19.6km (12¼ miles)
Total ascent	1350m (4420ft)
Grade	5
Walking time	8hrs
Terrain	Low fell paths; rocky ascents involving easy scrambling; high ridge walking on open fell; return by rough track and road
Maps	OS Explorer OL6; or OS Landrangers 89 and 90
Refreshments	Choice of pubs and cafés in Coniston
Transport	Bus 505, X12 and, summer only, X33

Leave the car park, turn left along the residential road – Ruskin Avenue – and, almost immediately, turn left along the B5285, passing the Crown Inn on your right. At the T-junction, turn left to cross the bridge and immediately take the narrow lane on the right. Turn right along the track straight after the Sun Hotel – signposted Old Man and Levers Water. Go through the gate near some farm buildings to access a rough track.

The track soon climbs beside the wooded ravine of **Church Beck**. Just after a waterfall, cross the beck via Miners Bridge and then turn left along the clear track, continuing upstream. About 150m after the bridge, turn right along a gently ascending track. Bear right at a fork to continue uphill and then, at the next junction in another 150m, turn right again. A wide carpet of grass leads temptingly into the disued quarry workings, but you should leave it just before it does so by turning left along a path climbing beneath the slate spoil heaps. (The beginning of this path is obscured by bracken in summer.)

On the summit of the Old Man with Low Water directly below

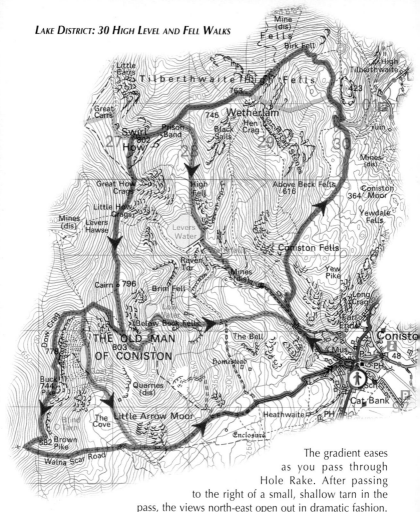

The gradient eases as you pass through Hole Rake. After passing to the right of a small, shallow tarn in the pass, the views north-east open out in dramatic fashion. The clear path descends but maintains enough height to avoid the boggy ground in the bottom of this hanging valley.

About 1.5km after the shallow tarn in Hole Rake – just as you approach the wooded ravine of Tilberthwaite Gill – drop left to carefully ford the rocky bed of Crook Beck. Swing right along a vague, sometimes damp path that soon reaches a wooden footbridge close to an open mine adit. After crossing, follow the stony trail up the embankment to a cairned junction of paths. Turn left, along the route of an old miners' track. This winds its way up into the mountains, through disused mine workings.

About 1km after joining the miners' track, it becomes a pitched path climbing above a small ruined building. After the pitching ends – and just beyond a short section on bare rock – don't be lured off course by a grassy trail to the right. You quickly reach the open ridge on **Birk Fell** where you're greeted by a magnificent panorama which includes the Fairfield and Helvellyn ranges as well as the craggy fells above Langdale. Swing left along the ridge towards Wetherlam Edge, Wetherlam's steep, north-east shoulder. The ensuing climb is steep and rocky all the way to the top of the mountain, and you will inevitably need to use your hands in places, to finally reach the summit cairn on **Wetherlam**.

Your efforts are rewarded by the sudden appearance of the **Coniston Fells**, including the Old Man. Standing on the summit, your eyes will also be drawn north-west to some of the Lake District's most impressive mountains: Crinkle Crags and Bow Fell can be seen in the middle distance; behind them are Scafell and Scafell Pike.

Head west-north-west across the rocky summit, a path slowly materialising as it drops slightly to traverse the northern flank of **Black Sails**. Drop to the large cairn at Swirl Hawse. The walk can be cut short by turning left at Swirl Hawse and then following the track down through the Coppermines Valley and back to Coniston.

From Swirl Hawse, continue straight across to climb the next ridge. This is **Prison Band**: it too is steep and rocky, but not as challenging as Wetherlam Edge. The summit of **Swirl How** is marked by a neat cairn from where you can see the coast and, on a clear day, the Isle of Man, Snowdonia, Northern Ireland and Dumfries and Galloway in Scotland.

Turn left along the high, windswept ridge, always keeping close to the plunging drop on your left. Over the next 2km, the path drops to **Levers Hawse** and then climbs slowly on to Brim Fell. As you begin the climb, make sure you keep to the wide path along the eastern edge of the fell and aren't tempted by a path to the right. Beyond the cairn on top of **Brim Fell**, continue on the clear path. The complex rock face over to the right belongs to Dow Crag, home to dozens of climbing and scrambling routes. Before long, you climb easily to the **Old Man**, the highest point in the range. The walk can be cut short from the top of the Old Man by taking the so-called 'tourist path' down the eastern side of the fell.

Looking back towards Swirl How on the path up to Brim Fell

From the trig pillar and summit platform, turn round and retrace your steps back along the ridge for about 100m. Reaching a fork, bear left. This path runs almost parallel with the main ridge path for a short while before swinging left to descend to Goat's Hawse. The path to the left at Goat's Hawse offers one final escape route. Linking up with the Walna Scar Road, it simply misses out the Dow Crag ridge.

Cross the pass and climb the slope opposite. The path leads straight to the summit rocks of **Dow Crag**, which involve some easy scrambling. (To avoid the scramble, simply go round to the right and pick your way across the boulders.)

For a glimpse down into Dow Crag's fearsome gullies and a chance of spotting climbers on its tremendous crags, keep close to the edge of the fell as you

continue south along the ridge. **Buck Pike** is passed and then, with Blind Tarn sitting below it, the final top of the day, **Brown Pike**. From here, you're able to look out along south Cumbria's estuaries fanning out into Morecambe Bay.

Descend the zig-zagging path from Brown Pike to a clear junction. Turn left here – along the **Walna Scar Road**. With far-reaching views to the east, follow this rough track steadily downhill for 3.4km – until you reach a gate at the road-end. Go through this and then continue downhill on the road. Turn left at the junction with Old Furness Road – effectively straight on. Take the next road on the left. Passing the Sun Hotel, retrace your steps to the car park, remembering to go left at the main road and then immediately right.

Walk 17

The Langdale Pikes

The Langdale Pikes are possibly the most recognisable group of fells in the Lake District. Their gnarly countenance towers over Great Langdale, creating a scene that is both dramatic and enticing. Who can stand firm against the lure of these mini-mountains? Despite the stiff climb to Stickle Tarn at the base of the pikes, it seems few walkers can resist. So you're unlikely to have the place to yourself as you continue upwards to explore the rocky tops of Pavey Ark (700m), Harrison Stickle (736m), Loft Crag (682m) and Pike o' Stickle (709m), but the popularity of the area won't detract from what is an excellent excursion on mostly good paths. In complete contrast to this craggy landscape, the route returns via peaty Martcrag Moor and the long valley of Mickleden.

The rocky dome of Pike o' Stickle from Loft Crag

Start/finish	National Trust pay-and-display car park at Old Dungeon Ghyll Hotel (NY 286 060)
Distance	12.1km (7½ miles)
Total ascent	855m (2800ft)
Grade	2/3
Walking time	5½hrs
Terrain	Open fell, rocky in places; steep ascent; easy scrambling on Pike o' Stickle can be avoided; boggy moorland; valley track
Maps	OS Explorer OL6; or OS Landranger 89 or 90
Refreshments	Old Dungeon Ghyll Hotel in Great Langdale
Transport	Bus 516, Langdale Rambler

Follow the access lane away from the Old Dungeon Ghyll car park and, where it swings left, go through the small gate on the right – signposted Mickleden and Stake Pass. Once through the gate at the top, turn right and, almost immediately, bear half-left to head up to another gate. Beyond this, follow the clear bridleway east along the base of the fells. Soon after a footbridge below a small waterfall, go through a gate and drop to a path junction next to Stickle Ghyll.

Turn left to walk upstream with the churning beck on your right. Cross via the next footbridge and then continue uphill with the water on your left. Keep right at an early fork as a trail heads left to ford the gill. Slightly

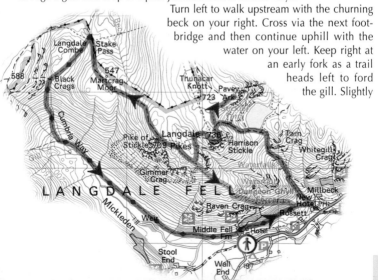

higher, bear left at a second fork, crossing a tiny slate bridge to climb a path cut through the rock. It's mostly on a well-constructed path, but it's a tough climb with some rocky sections. It later crosses Stickle Ghyll via some huge, well-placed boulders. Continuing upstream, keep left as you near **Stickle Tarn**.

It's hardly surprising that **Stickle Tarn** is one of the most visited high-level tarns in the Lake District: aside from being large enough to host countless summer picnics along its pleasant shores, it also occupies a striking mountain cirque. The crags of Harrison Stickle to the west are pretty impressive, but it is the daunting eastern face of Pavey Ark that commands all attention. A groove can be seen cutting across the rock face. This is Jack's Rake, one of Lakeland's most famous scrambling routes.

From the dam, walk with the tarn on your right for about 130m and then bear left to climb the gap between Harrison Stickle and Pavey Ark. The path is steep, particularly in its higher stages, but it's pitched for most of the way, making for a straightforward ascent. There'll be plenty of opportunities for stopping to take in the scale and complexity of Pavey Ark's cliff – and to gaze down on the tarn and its picnickers far below.

At a T-junction close to the top of the fells, turn right. (You'll return to this point after visiting Pavey Ark.) The path isn't always obvious as you weave your way in and out of rock outcrops and hop from boulder to boulder, but there are cairns leading the way. On reaching a few small, peaty pools, cross the tumble-down wall up to the right and make your way on to the summit rocks of **Pavey Ark**.

The **view from the top** includes Stickle Tarn below, the Helvellyn and Fairfield ranges to the east, Scafell Pike, Bow Fell, Wetherlam, Windermere and, in the distance, the distinctive rounded hills of the Howgills – part of the Yorkshire Dales National Park.

From the summit, retrace your steps to the T-junction at the top of the pitched path and then continue straight on – making a beeline for **Harrison Stickle**. Ignoring a cairned route to the right, keep to the most obvious path heading straight up to the base of the summit crags. This then veers left around the eastern side of the rocks and up to the summit.

In the higher reaches of Stickle Ghyll

Looking across Mickleden towards Bow Fell and Crinkle Crags

From the cairn marking the highest point on Harrison Stickle, the easiest way to descend is to drop west south-west initially. Thirty metres or so in this direction will bring you on to an indistinct path, along which you turn right (north north-west). Quickly reaching a cairn in a grassy gap, turn left (west). The path is faint at first but badly eroded lower down.

At the bottom of the slope, you'll reach a junction of paths. Ignoring the clear route heading out across boggy ground towards the prominent dome of Pike o' Stickle, head south-east for about 100m. As the path nears the beck, drop right to ford it. A clear path continues on the other side, but you should leave this after about 80m – by bearing right along a faint trail (south south-west). In another 80m or so, turn right (west) at an indistinct path junction marked by a large cairn. To cut short the walk, turn left here to follow the path down Mark Gate and back into Great Langdale. This descent is described in more detail in Walk 19.

The rocks to the left in a short while belong to Loft Crag. When the path forks, bear left up a loose, stony trail that soon swings right to reach the top of the fell and a tremendous view of Pike o' Stickle. Continue along the ridge in the direction of the rocky dome and you'll eventually reach a clear path close to the base of it. Turn left here.

As far as walkers are concerned, **Pike o' Stickle** is impenetrable on all but its north-east side, where a couple of easy scrambles lead to the top. For the easiest of these, take the narrow trail on the left immediately after climbing a few pitched steps. (Those who don't wish to lay their hands on rock can wait for their companions at this junction.) The well-used route is easy to make out and you're soon standing on the summit enjoying spectacular views across Mickleden towards Bow Fell.

Retrace your steps to the base of the scramble trail and turn left. Continue uphill for a few metres and then bear right at a fork. Parting company with the Langdale Pikes, the long return route begins now. Heading roughly north-west, a path begins descending – with Skiddaw visible in the distance. A constructed path seems to float on top of the horribly soggy expanse of **Martcrag Moor**. When it ends, continue north-west, descending damp moorland.

About 1.6km beyond Pike o' Stickle, you'll reach a T-junction in among grassy hummocks near **Stake Pass**. Turn left, following the narrow but obvious path as it weaves its way through **Langdale Combe** to the top of Stake Gill. Ford the beck and then begin a zig-zagging descent into the gorgeous valley of **Mickleden**. At a T-junction near a sheepfold, turn left to cross a bridge over **Stake Gill** and then follow the clear track downstream.

About 2.7km after joining the track, you will see **Middle Fell Farm** over the wall on the right. Now watch for the small gate you passed through at the beginning of the walk so that you can retrace your steps to the car park, remembering to turn left along the Old Dungeon Ghyll's access lane.

Walk 18

Pike o' Blisco and Crinkle Crags

The combination of Pike o' Blisco (705m) and Crinkle Crags (859m) makes for an incredible day out on the fells: a roller-coaster of high, rocky ground with a fine outlook in all directions. Pike o' Blisco is climbed first – on a good path culminating in a series of short, easy scrambles to reach the airy summit. The route then drops to Red Tarn before climbing steadily towards Crinkle Crags, a series of dramatic buttresses, scree gullies and gnarled, rocky peaks that tower over Great Langdale. The fell consists of five separate tops, with boulder-strewn interludes between them. The second involves a notorious 'bad step' scramble, which can be easily bypassed. Taking in Shelter Crags too, it's a tough ridge, and one that is best saved for a clear day, as it is easy to become disorientated. This walk can be combined with Walk 19 (joined at Three Tarns) to create a tough 17.7km circuit of Langdale.

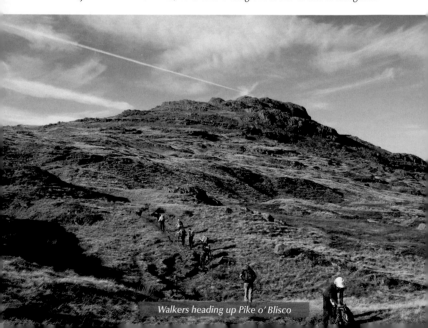

Walkers heading up Pike o' Blisco

Start/finish	Pay-and-display car park at Old Dungeon Ghyll Hotel (NY 286 060)
Distance	11.9km (7½ miles)
Total ascent	995m (3260ft)
Grade	3/4
Walking time	6½hrs
Terrain	Open fell, often rocky; easy scrambling on Pike o' Blisco; 'bad step' on Crinkle Crags can be avoided
Maps	OS Explorer OL6; or OS Landranger 89 or 90
Refreshments	Old Dungeon Ghyll Hotel in Great Langdale
Transport	Bus 516, Langdale Rambler

From the car park, head out on to the road and turn right. About 1km after leaving the car park, you reach some tight bends as the road begins climbing steeply. On the second sharp bend to the left, just after a small cutting with room for one car to park in it, take the path on the right. This isn't signposted, so you'll need to watch carefully for it.

Eventually emerging from the gill, the gradient briefly eases as the clear, cairned path makes its way towards the crags and boulders that crowd the summit of Pike o' Blisco. Later, things get trickier as you need to use your hands on four short scrambles. In

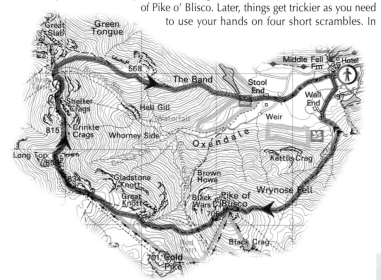

Three Tarns between Crinkle Crags and Bow Fell

winter, when these rocks are sheathed in ice, it is possible to avoid the most difficult sections by heading up to the left as you reach the base of each obstacle and then finding an easier route beside the rocks. If you do this, you must swing right again after each detour to return to the cairned path. The summit cairn and tiny shelter are on the north-west edge of the small, knobbly top of **Pike o' Blisco**. From here, there's a great bird's eye view down into Great Langdale and across to Crinkle Crags, your next target.

A well-used path, steep and stony in places, descends the other side of the fell: south south-west at first, soon veering south-west. At the bottom of the slope, as a path comes in from the left, keep straight on to cross the outlet stream of **Red Tarn** via stepping stones. The path, pitched again now, soon begins climbing.

The relatively dull stretch from the base of Pike o' Blisco to Crinkle Crags can be a bit of a slog, but your rewards are just around the next corner. Things get a lot more interesting when you have to clamber up on to the first Crinkle. The views, which include the magnificent Scafell range, become ever more impressive. The route along the top of the Crinkles is rocky in places, but as long as you stick to the main path, it shouldn't present the average fell-walker with any problems, except when it comes to the second Crinkle.

Having dropped from the first top into a stony saddle, you are faced with a choice. Straight ahead, at the top of a mess of scree, is the infamous 'bad step'. This is a tricky little climb if you're not used to scrambling. Alternatively, by bearing left at the base of the scree slope, you will find yourself on an easier, albeit

Looking towards the second Crinkle

steep route on to the summit. If you choose this route, make sure you bear right at the top of the climb, passing to the right of a tiny tarn – this will ensure you get back on to the ridge route and don't miss the summit of the second, and highest, of the Crinkles, also known as **Long Top**.

From the summit cairn, continue generally north along the line of rocky summits. It's rough underfoot and there are some bouldery areas to negotiate – but at no point is the cairned route exposed or scary.

Eventually, you descend from **Shelter Crags** to reach **Three Tarns**, at the bottom of the steep path on to Bow Fell. Turn right here: the path is clear once you're on it, but it's easy to miss because of the stony nature of the ground in this area.

The early, pitched part of the descent on to **The Band** is followed by a long, relatively level section and then more pitching as the gradient steepens again. The path eventually goes through a kissing-gate and then reaches a T-junction close to the valley bottom. Turn left and go through a gate to enter the farmyard at Stool End. Follow the waymarkers round to the right and out along the farm's access drive. Turn left along the Langdale road – effectively straight on. Take the next turning on the left and then bear right to return to the car park.

Walk 19

Bow Fell and the Mickleden Round

*Another grand day above Langdale. This is a relatively long, tough walk, but
the variety of terrain and scenery is hard to beat: put simply, it's wonderful!
Starting from the western end of Great Langdale, it completes a high-level
circuit of the valley through which Mickleden Beck runs. The Band provides a
relatively easy way on to the high fells, from where it's a short but stony climb
on to Bow Fell (902m) for a magnificent view of the Scafells. Dropping down
Ore Gap to Angle Tarn, the walk then ascends Rossett Pike (642m) at the head
of Mickleden. Coming off this boulder-strewn ridge, it crosses boggy, featureless
moorland near Stake Pass and then descends via Loft Crag and Mark Gate.*

Looking into Mickleden from Rossett Pike

Start/finish	Pay-and-display car park at Old Dungeon Ghyll Hotel (NY 286 060)
Distance	14.8km (9¼ miles)
Total ascent	1100m (3600ft)
Grade	3/4
Walking time	7½hrs
Terrain	Open fell, rocky in places, occasionally boggy
Maps	OS Explorer OL6; or OS Landranger 89 or 90
Refreshments	Old Dungeon Ghyll Hotel in Great Langdale
Transport	Bus 516, Langdale Rambler

From the car park, head out on to the road and turn right. When the road bends sharp left, keep straight ahead through the kissing-gate to access a surfaced farm track. On approaching **Stool End Farm**, follow the clear waymarkings, passing to the left of the farmhouse and then out of the farmyard through a large gate.

A track rises briefly beside the wall on your left. About 70m beyond the farm, turn right along a path

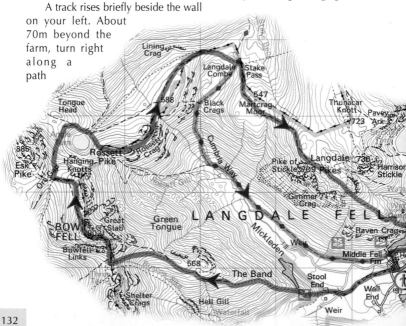

The Scafells from Bow Fell

heading uphill. It's a fairly steep climb on to the ridge known as **The Band**, but it's mostly on a pitched path, creating a relatively easy way on to the high fells.

In the early stages, you'll see **Pike o' Stickle** and its forbidding screes looming over Mickleden. Higher up, your attention is more likely to be grabbed by Crinkle Crags, dominating the head of Oxendale.

On approaching the saddle that houses **Three Tarns** and a magnificent first glimpse across to the Scafells, bear right to begin the tough climb on to Bow Fell. The path is steep and loose as it makes its way up through this rock-bound terrain, but the gradient quickly eases.

As you approach the spiky summit of **Bow Fell**, the path becomes indistinct. To reach the top, follow the line of cairns across the boulders. The best way to reach the highest point is to follow the cairns to the right of it and then approach it from the north-east. On the way across, it's worth detouring to the eastern side of the fell to see the Great Slab, an excellently inclined smooth chunk of volcanic ash.

Rossett Pike and the Langdale Pikes behind

Having bagged the top, drop down from the summit rocks the same way that you came up and then continue following the cairns. The general direction is north, although after the initial, steep descent to a shallow saddle, the path swings north north-west, keeping to the west of the highest, rocky ground.

About 1km beyond the summit, you drop into a pronounced dip between Bow Fell and Esk Pike. This is **Ore Gap**. Turn right on what is, at first, a clear path. As the gradient increases and the path crosses loose, stony ground, it is easy to lose sight of it, but there are cairns to guide you.

On reaching a junction with a clear, pitched path, turn right to drop to **Angle Tarn**. Cross the outlet stream and then climb the path directly ahead, ignoring a trail to the right and a clear path to the left. About 300m beyond the tarn, soon after the path levels off, turn left at a large cairn. The faint trail quickly climbs to the summit cairn on **Rossett Pike**.

Looming over the head of Mickleden, the minor peak of **Rossett Pike** gives some surprisingly far-reaching views, including the Forest of Bowland. Closer in, you can look across to the Great Slab on Bow Fell.

From the highest cairn, head south-east to a lower cairn on the eastern end of the summit ridge and then swing north-east. There isn't a path as such and the ground is rough and bouldery as you pick your way along the ridge-top. It's hard-going if you continue along the highest ground, but you will eventually meet a clearer, easier path. Alternatively, head slightly north to pick up this path at an earlier stage. Whichever route you take, the path eventually swings around the top of **Langdale Combe**. It is wet and peaty in places, but stepping stones have been conveniently placed to ease progress over the worst bits.

Soon after passing to the right of a small tarn, turn right along a clearer path and then, in a few more metres, keep left at a fork to begin climbing again. To cut short the walk, keep right at this fork and then follow the path down Stake Gill and into Mickleden. This is the descent route described in Walk 17.

The slopes of Martcrag Moor are often damp, so it's easy to lose the path. It heads generally south south-east. The terrain isn't terribly interesting, but if you need a bit of inspiration at this late stage of the day, simply turn round and soak up the panorama, taking in Rosthwaite Fell, Glaramara, Great Gable, Great End and Esk Pike. Eventually, you pick up a constructed path. When this ends, continue towards **Pike o' Stickle**. The path passes to the left of this great dome of rock; those who wish to 'bag' it will need to scramble to the summit (see Walk 17).

Descending from Bow Fell with the Scafells in the background

Just after Pike o' Stickle, you reach a cairn at the top of a steep scree chute. The clear path now swings left. Almost immediately, bear right on a less-travelled path along a short, grassy ridge on the western edge of the high ground. Just before this begins to climb on to Loft Crag, bear left at a small cairn to skirt the base of the crag – or bear right to climb to the summit and then swing left to drop back to the main path.

Continuing roughly south south-east beyond Loft Crag, you find yourself dropping off the fell on a steep, stony but cairned path, known as the Mark Gate route. This path – pitched in places, occasionally boggy and sometimes rocky – weaves its way down into Great Langdale. It's mostly clear on the ground, but where it's not, there are cairns to guide you.

At the end of the long descent, ford **Dungeon Ghyll** and bear right. Cross the stile and walk downhill with the wall on your left. At the bottom of the slope, turn right to follow a path along the base of the fell for about 800m. After going through a kissing-gate above the Old Dungeon Ghyll Hotel, turn left. At the bottom of the slope, go through another kissing-gate on your left. Follow the track and then the surfaced lane around the back of the hotel and down into the car park.

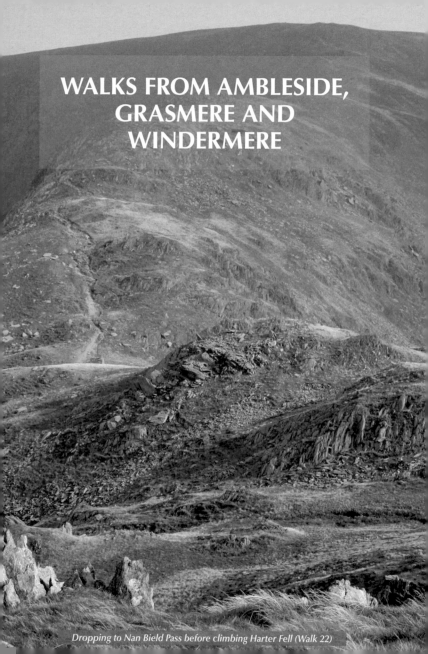

WALKS FROM AMBLESIDE, GRASMERE AND WINDERMERE

Dropping to Nan Bield Pass before climbing Harter Fell (Walk 22)

Walk 20

Fairfield Horseshoe

The Fairfield Horseshoe is one of the easiest of the classic Lakeland rounds, although, like any other fell walk, it should never be underestimated: it involves a fairly long day on the fells, most of it above the 600m contour, where the weather can be prone to sudden change. But those who come prepared will be in for a treat, particularly those who enjoy gazing off to distant horizons – because of its central location, the views of the rest of the Lake District are superb. Starting from Ambleside and ascending via Nab Scar, the route takes in Heron Pike (612m), Great Rigg (766m), Fairfield (873m), Hart Crag (822m), Dove Crag (792m), High Pike (656m) and Low Pike (508m).

Rocky ground on High Pike

Start/finish	Main car park in Ambleside, just N of the town centre on A591 (NY 375 047)
Distance	16.9km (10½ miles)
Total ascent	1050m (3450ft)
Grade	3
Walking time	6½hrs
Terrain	Valley track; open fell, mostly grassy but one or two stony sections and some peaty patches; town roads
Maps	OS Explorer OL5 and OL7; or OS Landranger 90
Refreshments	Choice of cafés and pubs in Ambleside; Old Schoolroom tea shop at Rydal Hall
Transport	Ambleside is served by a range of buses, including the 555.

From the car park, turn left along the main road – heading out of Ambleside. After almost 500m, you'll pass a bus stop. Soon after, carefully cross the road and go through the iron gates on the right – signposted Rydal Hall. A rough track skirts the base of grassy slopes, providing views of Nab Scar, Heron Pike and the western arm of the Fairfield Horseshoe. There are some fine old trees beside the track, indicative of this having once been parkland – part of the **Rydal Hall** estate.

Go through a large gate to enter the main grounds of the hall. Soon after the track swings left, turn right – signposted Rydal Mount, Coffin Route and Nab Scar. Immediately go straight across a track and make your way towards a white estate building. Turn left in front of it. The track winds its way uphill, passing The Old Schoolroom tea shop and then swinging left.

When the lane reaches a road, turn right, heading steeply uphill. Ignore the footpath to the left for Grasmere near Rydal Mount. At a fork, follow the concrete track up to the left. Then, as this

The ridge wall on the eastern arm of the Fairfield Horseshoe

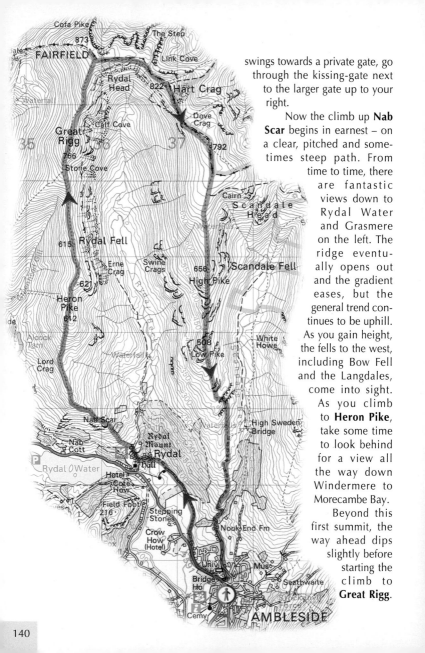

swings towards a private gate, go through the kissing-gate next to the larger gate up to your right.

Now the climb up **Nab Scar** begins in earnest – on a clear, pitched and sometimes steep path. From time to time, there are fantastic views down to Rydal Water and Grasmere on the left. The ridge eventually opens out and the gradient eases, but the general trend continues to be uphill. As you gain height, the fells to the west, including Bow Fell and the Langdales, come into sight. As you climb to **Heron Pike**, take some time to look behind for a view all the way down Windermere to Morecambe Bay.

Beyond this first summit, the way ahead dips slightly before starting the climb to **Great Rigg**.

Looking down the eastern arm towards Windermere

Walkers dropping into Link Hause with Hart Crag behind

From here, you can see the Helvellyn range to the north. Beyond Great Rigg, the ridge path drops again before climbing to **Fairfield**.

As you approach the first shelter on the flat summit area, look to your right. Take note of the path here, because you need to follow this off the top of the fell. But, before joining it, take some time to explore the summit of Fairfield – there are several shelters in which to take a break; and there are some magnificent views from the edges of the plateau, especially on the east side where you can look down on several imposing crags.

From the cross-shaped shelter on the eastern side of the summit, walk south-east to pick up the path you saw earlier, soon veering east. It drops into Link Hause and then climbs to **Hart Crag**. The path splits as the gradient eases near the summit rocks. As long as you don't drop left, you shouldn't go wrong. Faint trails through the rocks on the right head to the summit cairn, or you can keep to the main path which passes to the left of it.

Descending towards Ambleside at the end of the walk

From the top of Hart Crag, descend south-east, down a rocky path, to a dilapidated drystone wall. Keep this on your right as you head gently uphill to the top of **Dove Crag**. The ridge wall now guides you practically all the way back to Ambleside. Keep to the left of it. The descent south of Dove Crag is very gradual, although occasionally damp and peaty. After **High Pike**, however, there are several steep, rocky sections to negotiate. All the while, Windermere sparkles in the distance, calling you down from the hills.

About 3.3km beyond Dove Crag, the path swings away from the wall to bypass Sweden Crag. Later still, it passes through rough grazing land as it nears the edge of Ambleside. Cross Low Sweden Bridge and, just beyond this, go through a large wooden gate followed by a metal gate to join a sealed road at **Nook End Farm**.

Walk down the lane and, where it forks, bear right. At a T-junction, turn right. Turn left at the small roundabout. The pedestrian access to the car park is via the small bridge on the opposite side of the busy A591.

Walk 21

Helm Crag and Blea Rigg

This excellent excursion on to the mid-level fells to the west of Grasmere is best saved for a clear day when the impressive views can be fully appreciated and there's less chance of going astray on the sometimes complicated terrain. From Grasmere, the route first climbs steeply to the iconic summit of Helm Crag (405m) before heading north-west along a low ridge to Calf Crag (537m). The next stops are Codale Head and Sergeant Man (736m), reached via a less well-travelled trail up beside Mere Beck. The return route uses the long, broad and complex ridge of Blea Rigg.

The Howitzer on Helm Crag

Start/finish	Start of Easedale Road in Grasmere, opposite the Sam Read bookshop (NY 337 076)
Distance	15.1km (9½ miles)
Total ascent	880m (2890ft)
Grade	2
Walking time	5¾hrs
Terrain	Open fell, wet in places; indistinct paths at times
Maps	OS Explorer OL6 and OL7; or OS Landranger 90
Refreshments	Wide choice in Grasmere
Transport	Bus 555

From opposite the Sam Read bookshop in Grasmere, follow Easedale Road up the valley for 1.3km. Turn right at Jackdaw Cottage along a stone track – signposted Helm Crag. A few metres beyond a gate, take the walled path on the right, still following signs for Helm Crag.

Emerging from between the walls, turn right. Almost immediately, bear left along a well-walked path heading uphill through old quarry workings and then beside a wall. Later parting company with the wall, the path bends sharp left. Look up into Easedale, and you'll soon see the white streak of Sourmilk Gill slicing through the bedrock to the west.

There are other paths on to **Helm Crag**, but try to keep to the constructed path as much as possible: not only are you helping reduce erosion on this popular fellside, but, doing it this way makes the sudden appearance of Fairfield, to the east, all the more dramatic. Having reached this glorious viewpoint on the edge of the ridge, swing left to continue the climb. You soon encounter a fork. The left-hand route is the easier option, missing out the straightforward scrambling up to the first group

Seat Sandal, left, and Fairfield suddenly appear on the climb to Helm Crag

of rocks, known as the Lion and the Lamb. But the right-hand option is more
interesting, giving walkers a chance to look down on the fascinating jumble of
shattered rocks to the east of the ridge. Beyond the Lion and the Lamb, the paths
converge for the final climb towards the highest rocks on Helm Crag – the so-
called Howitzer. Experienced scramblers may wish to climb to the top of the
rocks; others will be satisfied with standing at the bottom of them and looking up.

From the Howitzer, the ridge path continues north-west. It drops steeply after
Helm Crag and then meanders up and over **Gibson Knott**. As long as you aren't
lured by lesser trails to the right, you'll eventually reach the cairn-topped summit
of **Calf Crag**. This is almost 3.2km north-west of Helm Crag, although, after all the
twists and turns and ups and downs of the ridge path, it'll feel further. The path
now heads north north-west, swinging west, to pass a few metres to the left of the
tarn at Brownrigg Moss.

At a cairn-marked junction at the head of Far Easedale, go straight across to
pick up a faint path (south-west). It's possible to cut the walk short here by turning
left and walking back through Far Easedale to Grasmere.

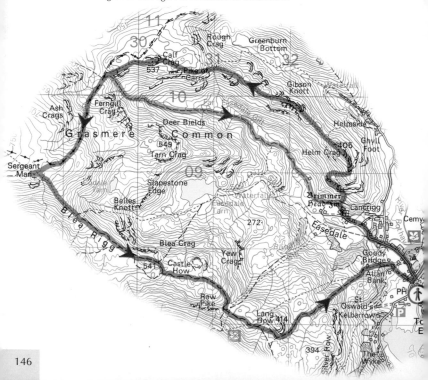

Pavey Ark and, far beyond that, the Coniston Fells glimpsed from near Sergeant Man

It's easy to lose sight of this trail where it crosses damp ground; the key is never to stray too far from the line of rusty old fenceposts. Mere Beck becomes a lively companion in the middle section of the ascent, but it's the fenceposts that will lead you unerringly towards Codale Head.

You'll know when you've reached Codale Head because a wonderful panorama of mountains suddenly appears ahead, including the Coniston Fells, Crinkle Crags and Bow Fell. Closer in – just 300m to the south-west – is the distinctive summit of Sergeant Man. Make your way towards the base of this, passing to the left of a wet depression on the way. On reaching a path just to the east of the summit, turn right for a short, easy clamber to the top of **Sergeant Man**, or turn left to continue on the main route.

The route on to **Blea Rigg** heads generally south-east, enjoying a superb view of Pavey Ark, Harrison Stickle and Stickle Tarn to the right. Having descended about 800m from Sergeant Man – just as you catch your first glimpse of Easedale Tarn down to the left – there is a fork marked by a small cairn. Bear right here, crossing the ridge and soon descending slightly. To ensure you don't end up in Langdale,

147

you must regain the high ground, marked by small cairns, immediately afterwards – heading south-east.

After a boggy area, you encounter some of the most rugged terrain on the ridge – along the top of **Blea Crag**. Look down to the left, and you'll see you are drawing level with the western end of Easedale Tarn. Don't be tempted by a path dropping left here.

Soon after passing to the left of a small tarn, you get your first view of Grasmere. Then, dropping from Little Castle How, the path swings right – heading to the right of a large damp area at Swinescar Hause. You'll see a tiny, stone enclosure up to the right as it swings left again. Where the main route then goes left at the south-east corner of the bog, continue straight on (south south-east) along a fainter trail.

Soon after passing the grassy, cairn-topped summit of Swinescar Pike, keep to the clear path that passes to the left of a large, reedy tarn. At the eastern end of the tarn, close to a tiny pool, bear left at a cairn to drop to the third body of water in quick succession. At its northern tip, bear left along the clearest path (north-east), keeping close to the base of **Lang How** up to your left at first. The path then skirts the northern edge of the worst of Brigstone Moss. When it peters out, keep straight on, across damp ground. The path soon becomes clearer and heads east north-east, later dropping through an area of juniper.

On reaching a stony path, turn left. As you briefly follow a small beck downstream, you can see Helm Crag straight ahead. At the bottom of the steep descent, bear right. The path is soon channelled, via a kissing-gate, between drystone walls. Turn right on reaching a surfaced lane. Passing below **Allan Bank**, follow this lane round to the left and back into Grasmere. Allan Bank, now a National Trust property, was the home of William Wordsworth and his family from 1808 to 1811. Go left at the road junction and you'll soon see the Sam Read bookshop, where the walk started, on the right.

Walk 22

Kentmere Round

The Kentmere Round is one of the Lake District's classic horseshoe routes – and one of its toughest. Visiting Yoke (706m), Ill Bell (757m), Froswick (720m), Harter Fell (778m) and Kentmere Pike (730m), it gives walkers a long day of spectacular ridge walking in wild, remote country on the south-east edge of the National Park. All of the paths are well walked, so there shouldn't be any problems with navigation – although the descent does cross some boggy ground. The drop from Shipman Knotts includes some straightforward rock steps.

Small Water and, left, High Street, from the climb to Harter Fell

Start/finish	Parking for a few cars beside the Kentmere Institute (NY 456 041), opposite the church. Small donation requested
Distance	19.5km (12 miles)
Total ascent	1075m (3530ft)
Grade	3/4
Walking time	7¼hrs
Terrain	Open fell with high ridge paths; generally grassy, occasionally boggy and also some rocky areas
Maps	OS Explorer OL7; or OS Landranger 90
Refreshments	None in Kentmere; nearest in Staveley
Transport	None
Alternative parking	An early start is recommended because there is very little other parking in Kentmere. Cars are sometimes allowed to park in a field (with honesty box) near Low Bridge (NY 458 039), about 200m SE of the Kentmere Institute.

With your back to the tiny Kentmere Institute building, turn left along the road. Follow it round a sharp left bend and then, when the asphalt ends, bear right along the 'restricted byway' – signposted Troutbeck via Garburn Pass. The initial climb up the Garburn Road, which passes above Kentmere Hall, isn't pleasant. Originally a drove road, the route has become badly eroded over the years and you'll sometimes end up crossing piles of loose rocks while dodging the mountain-bikers hurtling down from the pass.

The **Garburn Pass** itself is reached just beyond a gate and heralded by grand fell views to the west. Continue for a few more metres, dropping slightly, and

then, just before the track swings left, turn right along a stony path. Soon broadening, the path later joins the ridge wall, crosses it via a kissing-gate and then climbs to the first peak of the day: **Yoke**.

From the top of Ill Bell, the head of Kentmere appears through the clouds

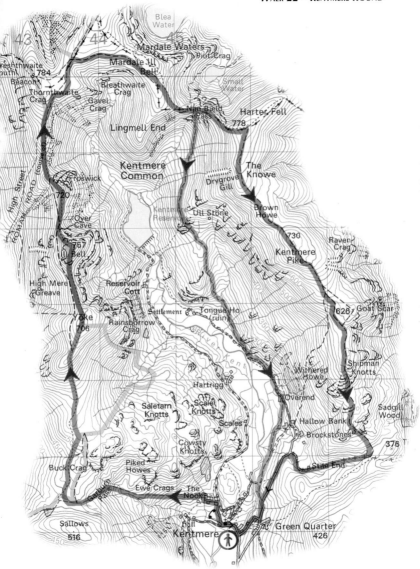

The ridge path leads on to Ill Bell

The top of **Yoke** is unremarkable, but the views are stunning. Looking ahead, you can see Ill Bell, High Street, Helvellyn and Fairfield; to the right is the eastern arm of the Kentmere Round, your return route.

From the continuing ridge path – with its dramatic, bird's-eye perspective on the upper reaches of the Kentmere valley – the more shapely peak of **Ill Bell** now beckons. Its prominent summit cairns are quickly reached. With wisps of cloud blowing around the airy summit, hiding then revealing startling glimpses down the mountain's steep eastern slopes, this can be a wonderfully atmospheric spot to linger. The route drops steeply from here and then begins the easier pull on to **Froswick**, always keeping to the clear ridge path.

From the top of Froswick, continue north over a grassy col. The ridge path then heads towards **Thornthwaite Crag**. Several hundred metres short of its summit, turn right at a pair of rusty old fenceposts – along a clear path. Bear right at two faint forks. There are a couple of heart-stopping moments as the loose, stony path, doing its best impersonation of a roller-coaster, negotiates a steep-sided gully. Otherwise, the narrow path is a delight, hugging the edge of the fell.

BORDER TROUBLES

Like many medieval buildings in Cumbria, Kentmere Hall features a defensive tower with incredibly thick walls. Known as a pele tower, it was built in the 14th century – at a time when Scottish raiding parties were ransacking the region. Wealthy families built themselves these stout, sturdy refuges attached to their homes and, in the event of an attack, would move in – often accompanied by their livestock. Today, pele towers, like the one at Kentmere Hall (pictured), are used mostly for agricultural purposes; others, such as at Muncaster Castle near Ravenglass, have been incorporated into large stately homes.

After a period of relative peace between the two nations, Edward I's determination in the 13th century to impose English sovereignty on Scotland kick-started a resurgence in border difficulties. This continued long after his death on the Solway marshes in 1307. In the early part of the 14th century, Robert the Bruce led Scottish raiding parties that got as far, in 1322, as Preston in north Lancashire. They burned entire towns, destroyed churches and slaughtered villagers, returning north with plunder and prisoners.

This was also the time of the Border Reivers – the ruthless clans who carried out cross-border raids, looting and pillaging, and bringing new, bleak words to the English language such as 'bereaved' and 'blackmail'. These families of the border's 'Debateable Lands' owed their allegiance to neither England nor Scotland. Their loyalty was to their clan names – names that still dominate local phone books: Beattie, Armstrong, Little, Storey, Turnbull, Graham...

The ground on the right drops away to the River Kent and **Kentmere Reservoir**, built in 1845 to regulate the supply of water to the mills further downstream.

Almost 2km after you first joined it at the old fenceposts, the path swings away from the edge. Keep left as a narrow trod heads right. On reaching a clearer path just below the top of **Mardale Ill Bell**, turn right. With superb views of Haweswater and occasional glimpses of Small Water below, descend to **Nan Bield Pass**. This dramatic gap in the ridge, one of the highest of the major Lake District passes, is home to a sturdy shelter. To cut short the walk, turn right at Nan Bield Pass and follow the bridleway back to Kentmere.

From the shelter, continue uphill to **Harter Fell**. Keep to the clearest path, straight up the rocky front of the fell, and you'll reach the summit, marked by a cairn with bits of metal sticking out of it. The panorama to the north-east now includes Cross Fell, the highest point on the Pennines.

Turn right to walk beside the fence on your left. A fence or wall will be your companion for several kilometres, providing a navigational aid in misty conditions. The only times the path deviates from its clear line are to avoid boggy areas and to cut a corner on Goat Scar. First though, it climbs **Kentmere Pike**. The trig pillar is on the east side of the wall, so it's easy to miss. The wall/fence soon goes out on to the top of **Goat Scar**, but the path cuts a corner. (Don't be tempted by a right fork here, dropping into Kentmere.) Rejoin the ridge wall at a ladder stile. Cross this and continue along the clear path. The descent becomes steeper and rockier as you drop from **Shipman Knotts**.

Turn right on reaching a clear, broad track at the bottom of the ridge. Go left when you reach a minor road, take the next road on your right and then turn right again at the T-junction to return to the church and the Kentmere Institute.

WALKS FROM THE
ULLSWATER AREA

The ridge wall on Hartsop Dodd (Walk 26)

Walk 23
Helvellyn via the edges

From its 950m summit, Helvellyn throws out two fine arêtes: Striding Edge and Swirral Edge. The former, in particular, has a fearsome reputation and has been the scene of many accidents over the years. Narrow in places and with lots of exposed rock, in winter conditions these two arêtes should be tackled only by experienced mountaineers. On a calm, dry day, on the other hand, they are well within the capabilities of walkers who have a head for heights and don't mind a bit of easy scrambling. Striding Edge, in particular, offers a superb and unforgettable high-level approach to England's third highest mountain. The descent along Swirral Edge also takes in Catstye Cam (890m), a wonderfully airy summit often bypassed by walkers.

On Striding Edge

Start/finish	Main pay-and-display car park in Glenridding (NY 385 169)
Distance	12.9km (8 miles)
Total ascent	915m (3000ft)
Grade	3/4
Walking time	5hrs
Terrain	Well-used fell paths on ascent and descent; two narrow, rocky ridges involving easy scrambling
Maps	OS Explorer OL5; or OS Landranger 90
Refreshments	Choice of pubs and cafés in Glenridding
Transport	Bus 508

From the car park, head on to the main road and turn right. Turn right again along a surfaced lane immediately after crossing Glenridding Beck – signposted Mires Beck, Helvellyn. Bear right at a fork in the track, continuing beside the beck. On reaching a minor road, turn left and then, almost immediately, pick up the gravel path to the right of the road. This soon joins a wider track as it heads uphill. On reaching a junction of tracks at a gate, keep straight on (left-hand option). In another 100m, you'll see a gate ahead; just before reaching it, fork right.

The clear track soon climbs to a gate. Go through this and cross the plank bridge on the left. Climb beside Mires Beck, soon crossing to the eastern bank via a ford. Although it's a straightforward path, it can be a bit of a slog at first, but then you reach the ridge and are met by a glorious sight: the dark gullies and airy ridges along the north-western face of St Sunday Crag. To the right of this are the cliffs of Fairfield.

The path continues uphill, soon beginning a zig-zagging ascent. Leave the path briefly to take a 650m there-and-back

On Birkhouse Moor with the pyramidal Catstye Cam behind and Helvellyn to the left of it

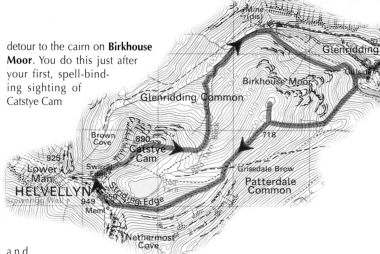

detour to the cairn on **Birkhouse Moor**. You do this just after your first, spell-binding sighting of Catstye Cam

and Helvellyn's eastern cliffs – and just before the path swings left. At this point, to reach the cairn, turn right along a faint, grassy trail.

Having visited the cairn, return to the main path and continue uphill, soon striding out with a wall to your left. Soon after passing – and ignoring – a ladder stile, you lose the wall on the left and continue straight ahead towards the start of **Striding Edge**.

You can either stick to the exciting, rocky apex of this narrow arête, scrambling easily over one or two small dips along the spine, or you can use the more straightforward path to the right of the rocks. With the ground dropping away steeply on either side and spectacular views in all directions, the more adventurous will get a better sense of the narrowness of the ridge – as well as a greater feeling of exhilaration – by choosing the former. A memorial on the south side of the ridge, overlooking Nethermost Cove, tells of the fatal fall from these rocks of local huntsman Robert Dixon in 1858.

The biggest difficulty on Striding Edge comes in the form of a rock tower, which has to be down-climbed with care. It can be avoided by using the narrow path to the left of the rocks, but this too has its difficulties, including a greater sense of exposure above a potentially long, steep drop. Having crossed the narrow ridge and negotiated the rock tower, the sting in Striding Edge's tail is the final climb on to Helvellyn's summit plateau. It's not technically difficult or exposed, but it is steep and, in places, loose – a far-from-fitting finale to what is otherwise a grand mountain approach.

At the top of this final climb, bear right along the edge of the fell, gazing down on Red Tarn all the while. You'll quickly pass another memorial plaque before swinging left to climb to the substantial summit shelter, summit cairn and then the trig pillar on Helvellyn.

LAKELAND TEARDROPS

There are literally hundreds of tarns scattered throughout the Lake District. The Norsemen who dominated the area 1000 years ago gave them their name: coming across small pools in the mountains, they called them tjorns – 'little lakes' or, literally, 'teardrops'. Most of them are remnants of the last glacial period when huge ice sheets scoured out hollows in the mountains, which then filled with water. Today, becks pouring down from the surrounding fells continue to fill the tarns, many of which feed into lakes and rivers in the valley bottoms.

It is hard to say exactly what a tarn looks like: it could be anything from a necklace of pools sparkling like blue jewels on high, lonely ridge tops to a small 'lake' sitting cold and moody at the base of sombre cliffs. Some say that a tarn must have a permanent outflow to justify being defined as such. Many of the walks in this book pass close to a tarn or two, including Seathwaite Tarn, Styhead Tarn, Bowscale Tarn, Innominate Tarn, Stickle Tarn and countless unnamed bodies of water.

The climb on to Helvellyn via its two arêtes does an almost complete circuit of Red Tarn – at almost 720m above sea level, one of the highest tarns in the Lake District. Sitting at the base of the cliffs of Helvellyn's east face and cradled between Striding Edge and Swirral Edge, it is also one of the best examples of a corrie tarn in the entire Lake District.

The exit from Striding Edge is marked by a plaque telling the story of **Charles Gough**, whose body was found in 1805 at the base of the crags beneath this spot. His rotting remains had been guarded for three months by his dog, a story that inspired Sir Walter Scott to write the poem *Climbed the Dark Brow of Mighty Helvellyn* and William Wordsworth to pen *Fidelity*.

The top of England's third highest mountain may be one of the busiest summits in the Lake District, if not the country, but it's still a marvellous spot to linger

On Catstye Cam, looking back along Swirral Edge to Helvellyn

on a clear day. The views, needless to say, are extensive. When you can tear yourself away from this magical spot, continue beyond the trig pillar to a sprawling cairn on the edge of the fell. This marks the start of the path down to **Swirral Edge**. Carefully descend the loose stones on the right to begin crossing the ridge. With less exposed rock and more obvious erosion, this isn't anywhere near as much fun as Striding Edge, but it still makes for an exciting descent.

About 500m after leaving Helvellyn's summit, don't be tempted by the clear path trending right, down towards Red Tarn; instead, keep to the ridge path and follow it up to the spiky, exposed summit of **Catstye Cam**. No broad, Helvellyn-like plateau here; just an airy perch on top of a pyramid-shaped peak. From the top, take the path heading south-east, veering east. When this peters out near the base of Catstye Cam, continue in roughly the same direction to reach the clear, well-trodden Red Tarn track. Turn left to follow this down into the valley of Glenridding Beck, crossing two bridges over tributary becks along the way.

About 200m after passing and ignoring a bridge over Glenridding Beck close to the converted mine buildings at Greenside, you will see a faint, grassy path to the left. Keep right here, staying on a superb, high-level path that follows the line of a disused leat.

The leat would have been used to carry water to power the workings at **Greenside lead mine**. The mine was the first in Britain to use electrical winding and underground haulage, generating its own electricity by means of water turbines.

Do not leave the leat path until you come to a low wall apparently blocking your way ahead. Bear left here to descend a rocky path. Turn right at the bottom of the short descent. Go through a gate and, retracing your steps from the start of the walk, follow the track down to a lane. Turn left along this and then turn right along a wide track just before the bridge over the beck. This leads back into Glenridding.

Red Tarn

Walk 24

Deepdale Round

Using Patterdale as its base, this superb horseshoe route climbs St Sunday Crag (841m) and the airy Cofa Pike on the way up to Fairfield (873m). The return is via Hart Crag (822m) and then along the lonely ridge of Hartsop above How. You'll need a full day for this – and not just because it's long. You'll also want time to savour the views, particularly across to the Helvellyn range from St Sunday Crag's wonderful ridge; you'll want time to explore the summit of Fairfield and gaze down on the spectacular crags of its northern face; and you'll inevitably want time, at the end of the route, to linger over that final, grassy spur.

Looking back to St Sunday Crag from Fairfield

Start/finish	George Starkey Hut, Patterdale (NY 394 160). There is room for a few cars to park in front of the building. Alternatively, the pay-and-display car park is 200m to the SE.
Distance	15.5km (9½ miles)
Total ascent	1025m (3370ft)
Grade	3/4
Walking time	5¼hrs
Terrain	Open fell, mostly with well-defined ridge paths; loose, stony descent; peaty, less clear on return section; valley paths
Maps	OS Explorer OL5; or OS Landranger 90
Refreshments	White Lion Inn and Patterdale Hotel, both in Patterdale
Transport	Bus 508

With your back to the George Starkey Hut in Patterdale, turn right along the main road, soon passing St Patrick's Church on your left. Take the next road on your left – a dead-end lane into **Grisedale**. Follow this uphill, ignoring the first footpath to the left near some cottages. Continue uphill for a further 400m and then go through a gate next to a fingerpost on your left.

A track climbs for about 70m and then swings right – through a small gate. Go straight over the path on the other side to begin climbing the fell. Soon after going through a gate in a wall, the gradient eases briefly, and you are able to enjoy the spectacular views across the valley to the coves and crags of Dollywaggon Pike, Nethermost Pike and Helvellyn. Immediately below is beautiful Grisedale. The path is mostly stony, but it does have a tendency to vanish on the boggy stretches. When this

On the way to St Sunday Crag

Dollywaggon Pike from St Sunday Crag

happens, keep heading south-west and, within a few strides, the path should magically reappear.

At the base of St Sunday's main ridge, keep right at a fork. Before long the fells to the west appear – Bow Fell, the Scafell group, Crinkle Crags and, finally, closer in, Fairfield. Make your way across the rock-strewn plateau to the highest point of **St Sunday Crag**.

Continue down the other side of the ridge. The complex group of dark crags over to the left – on the other side of Deepdale – belongs to Fairfield. The superb ridge path drops into **Deepdale Hause** and then climbs again – on to **Cofa Pike**. To cut short the walk, turn right at Deepdale Hause and descend to Grisedale Tarn. From here, follow the valley path back to Patterdale.

At the base of the steepest, rockiest part of the ascent, you have a choice: either keep left and climb straight up the ridge front, or bear right on the more long-winded route. The latter is still steep and rocky in places, but it is easier. At the top of this section, Cofa Pike's summit cairn is just ahead on the left; alternatively, bear right to skirt this narrow part of the ridge. Either way, you'll soon have to cross another short section of rocky ridge.

The path splits again on the final push to the summit of Fairfield. The most direct route is to the left, but this is very loose; if you take the gentler, right-hand branch, you'll need to swing left about 100m beyond the fork to reach the summit.

The top of **Fairfield** is a wide, flat expanse with magnificent views – now including Windermere and Morecambe Bay to the south. With so many cairns and shelters dotted about, it's easy to lose your bearings up here. From the cross-shaped shelter on the eastern side of the summit, your path is the broad, cairned route heading south-east, soon veering east. It drops to Link Hause and then climbs easily to **Hart Crag**.

To locate the path on to **Hartsop above How**, it is best to continue all the way to Hart Crag's summit

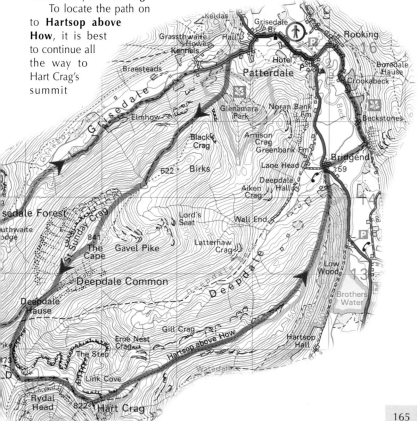

cairn, located among a jumble of angular boulders. (This is not the cairn to the left of the path at the top of the initial climb.) The path splits as the gradient eases near the summit rocks. Follow any one of several faint trails through the rocks on the right to reach the true top.

From the summit cairn on Hart Crag, retrace your steps for about 40m and then take the narrow path to the right (east north-east). It soon becomes clearer and stonier as it descends more steeply. When the gradient briefly eases, watch for a small cairn indicating a path to the right. You have a choice of descents here: either keep to the main path (left) and scramble down the rocky ridge, or bear right and take your chances on the steep, scree-like alternative. The two routes reunite after about 450m.

Having got the toughest part of the descent out of the way, the lovely ridge stretching out ahead of you now is Hartsop above How. It's a straightforward undertaking, your stride interrupted only by the occasional peaty patch. The ridge is broad enough to accommodate one or two deviations from the main path around boggy bits, but narrow enough to make it difficult for walkers to go seriously astray. The mesmerising panorama of ridges and valleys to the east guides you unerringly onwards.

Having lowered yourself down a rocky section, ignore the ladder stile on the right. Eventually, you reach a wall cutting across the fell; climb the ladder stile here to continue descending. The path runs roughly parallel with the ridge wall until you encounter some trees: now, as you cross the line of an old wall, swing left to reach a gate. Beyond this, make your way through the trees to the next gate. Go through this and follow a series of waymarker posts across the field (northwest). Turn right along a rough track and descend to the A592 at Deepdale Bridge.

Turn left along the road and, in 80m, take the track on the right. This ends at some gates. Go through the kissing-gate and follow the curving path across the field to a gate in a fence. Go straight across the second field. In the third field, aim for the gate in the far right-hand corner and then turn left along the track. Having crossed **Goldrill Beck**, keep left at a track junction – signposted Patterdale. The track narrows after passing through a metal gate immediately after the buildings at **Beckstones**. Follow it through the yard at the next set of buildings – at **Crookabeck**.

Turn left on reaching a surfaced lane and then go right at the main road to walk back into Patterdale and to the George Starkey Hut.

Walk 25

Caiston Glen Round

There's something very pleasing, in a visual sense, about the way Hartsop's 'Dodds' rise unerringly skyward at the far end of Patterdale. Each of their smooth, grassy slopes, largely uninterrupted by crags, climbs from the valley to the high fells in one short, sharp pull. This walk ascends the energy-sapping ridge of Middle Dodd (654m) and then comes down High Hartsop Dodd (519m). In between, it climbs on to Red Screes (776m), a superb place to linger and take in the excellent 360-degree views.

Middle Dodd from the valley

Start/finish	Car park at Cow Bridge on A592 near Brothers Water (NY 402 133)
Distance	10.8km (6¾ miles)
Total ascent	800m (2620ft)
Grade	2/3
Walking time	4½hrs
Terrain	Valley track and paths; open fell, mostly grassy; steep ascent and descent; upland paths not always clear
Maps	OS Explorers OL5 and OL7; or OS Landranger 90
Refreshments	Brotherswater Inn, 1.6km S of Hartsop
Transport	Bus 508 (serves Cow Bridge summer only)

From the car park, go through the gate and walk along a broad, gravel track with the water on your left. Having passed **Brothers Water**, you reach the buildings of **Hartsop Hall**.

The first **hall** at Hartsop was built in the 12th century when the Normans used the valley as a hunting forest. The land passed to the Lowther family by marriage in the 15th century, and the hall was rebuilt. Much of the current structure, which now belongs to the National Trust, dates from the 16th century.

Immediately after passing the buildings on your left, the track swings left and then right – as if making for the stone barns to the south of the hall. Leave the track before it reaches

The barn at the base of High Hartsop Dodd

those buildings by quickly bearing left across a foot-bridge – signposted Kirkstone Pass and Scandale Pass – and then going through a small gate in the wall. Turn right and, in 70m, as you reach the far end of the buildings on your right, swing left (south south-east) to make for the wide bridge across **Dovedale Beck**. Then continue in roughly the same direction, making for a stone barn at the bottom of the ridge leading up to **High Hartsop Dodd**.

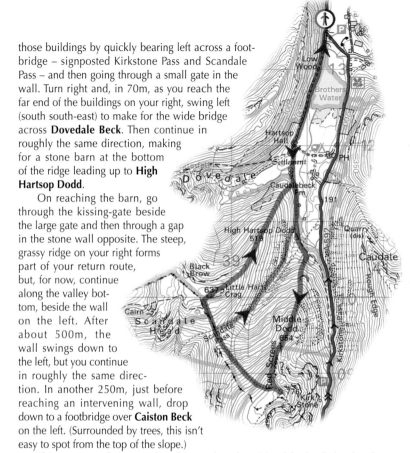

On reaching the barn, go through the kissing-gate beside the large gate and then through a gap in the stone wall opposite. The steep, grassy ridge on your right forms part of your return route, but, for now, continue along the valley bottom, beside the wall on the left. After about 500m, the wall swings down to the left, but you continue in roughly the same direction. In another 250m, just before reaching an intervening wall, drop down to a footbridge over **Caiston Beck** on the left. (Surrounded by trees, this isn't easy to spot from the top of the slope.)

There isn't an obvious path at first on the other side of the beck, but head south south-east for about 80m and you'll pick up a narrow, stony path. As soon as this crosses a tumbledown wall, turn right to begin the ascent of Middle Dodd. There's no path on the ground at first as you slowly climb beside the wall on your right, but as soon as you've passed the prominent crag on your left, swing over on to the ridge proper (left) and you'll pick up a good path. This crosses a tumbledown wall as it continues ascending. It's very steep but the path seems always to pick the best line, which becomes particularly relevant as you pass through a rocky area near the top.

Looking back down the ridge towards Middle Dodd from the top of Red Screes

When you reach the summit cairn on **Middle Dodd**, there's a moment of relief that the climb is finally over, but this is tempered by the appearance of the sweeping ridge leading up on to **Red Screes**. This holds the promise of more uphill work, but, rest assured, this climb isn't anywhere near as hard as the one

just completed. As you continue along the clear ridge path and begin ascending again, the vista just keeps getting better, particularly to the west where more and more of the Lake District's highest mountains are appearing, including Crinkle Crags, Bow Fell, Scafell, Scafell Pike and Great Gable.

The summit of **Red Screes** is marked by a trig pillar. From here, you can see quite some way south – across Morecambe Bay and as far as Blackpool Tower on a clear day.

From the trig pillar, turn round and, almost heading back on yourself, take the path north north-west, soon swinging west. At a junction of tumbledown walls, turn right to head more steeply downhill.

Having dropped into **Scandale Pass**, continue straight up the other side – still with the wall on your left. To cut short the walk, turn right at Scandale Pass and follow Caiston Beck downstream until you regain your outward route close to the point at which it crossed the beck earlier.

It's easy to go astray at the top of the first climb – as the path swings away from the wall. Before the route starts climbing again, there is a faint fork. Keep right here – along the clearest path, keeping to the right of a line of redundant fenceposts. Halfway up the slope, bear right at a second fork, heading directly for **Little Hart Crag**. At the top of the next climb, pause a moment to take in the great view across Hartsop Above How to St Sunday Crag and then turn right along a stony path. A cairn, marking Little Hart Crag's highest point, is quickly reached.

A path continues along the ridge to a second cairn. After this, keep left at any forks and you soon drop to a clearer, grassy path. Bear right here to walk out along a gorgeous, rounded ridge. After a small cairn marking the top of **High Hartsop Dodd**, the path gets a bit steeper. After crossing a wall, it steepens again. Then, as you enter the only rocky area on the ridge, it steepens yet more. Basically, it's tough on the knees all the way to the valley bottom, but the impressive view of Brothers Water provides considerable consolation.

After crossing a stile in a fence, the final part of the descent is mostly on grass.

Take some time to look for the **Bronze Age settlement** in the field to the north of the barn below. You will have passed through the middle of it at the start of the walk, but it's just a muddle of lumps and bumps at ground level; seen from above, the outline of old walls is a lot more obvious.

When you finally reach the barn, go back through the gap in the wall and then the kissing-gate to retrace your steps. After the gate and narrow footbridge, don't forget to turn right and immediately left around the back of Hartsop Hall. This track will now return you to the car park.

Walk 26

Hartsop Dodd and Gray Crag

*This walk links two superb, mostly grassy ridges above the village of Hartsop:
Hartsop Dodd (618m) to the west of Pasture Beck and Gray Crag (710m) to the
east. It tackles Hartsop Dodd first – a steep, but enjoyable climb in magnificent
surroundings. To reach the second of the two ridges, the route plummets
from Stony Cove Pike (763m) into Threshthwaite Mouth – a steep, rocky
descent – and then climbs, almost as steeply, to the beacon on Thornthwaite
Crag (784m). The quiet path that then heads north along Gray Crag's lovely,
broad ridge provides a relaxing way to conclude another great day on high.*

Looking across the valley to Hartsop Dodd from near Thornthwaite Crag

Start/finish	Parking area at eastern end of Hartsop (NY 410 131)
Distance	9.5km (6 miles)
Total ascent	840m (2760ft)
Grade	2/3
Walking time	4½hrs
Terrain	Open fell, mostly grassy; rocky ground in Threshthwaite Mouth; steep ascents and descents
Maps	OS Explorer OL5; or OS Landranger 90
Refreshments	Brotherswater Inn, 1.6km S of Hartsop
Transport	Bus 508 (serves Cow Bridge summer only)

Go through the kissing-gate at the far end of the Hartsop car park and turn right – signposted **Pasture Beck**. Once over the bridge, a rough track climbs alongside a wall to a gate. Beyond these, the track swings left, but you leave it here by heading straight up the fellside beside the wall on your right. Cross a step stile in a wall corner and continue straight up the hill on a faint path beside the wall.

On reaching the ridge, you can see across to Dovedale and down to Brothers Water below. Turn left to climb a faint, grassy trail heading straight up the north ridge of **Hartsop Dodd**. It's a relentlessly steep climb, but you are surrounded by magnificent scenery with clear views on both sides of the ridge as well as back down to Hartsop.

Looking towards Hartsop above How and Fairfield from Hartsop Dodd

NOT JUST 'ANOTHER CROW'

Ravens get a bad press – for centuries they have been regarded as a bird of ill omen and walkers who spot them on the fells often dismiss them as 'just another crow'. And yet, researchers have discovered they are one of the most intelligent bird species on the planet. They have shown examples of playful behaviour and problem-solving abilities. In North America, for example, when they can't open an animal carcass to get at the meat inside, ravens have been known to call wolves and coyotes to the site so that the animals do the hard work for them.

There are Raven Crags all over the Lake District – including one on Hartsop Dodd – places where the birds nest or have been known to nest. They build a home of twigs, soil and moss, lined with softer materials such as grass and wool. They mate for life and will stay in the same area all that time, fiercely defending their territory.

Walkers may become aware of their presence when they hear the 'krorp' sound that these enormous black birds sometimes make in flight. They also have a 'crack-crack-crack' alarm call and make all sorts of other unusual noises – like many of their relatives in the crow family, the birds are good mimics.

Their aerobatic displays are particularly impressive. With a couple of lazy beats of the wings, the birds gain height and then plummet earthward, performing all sorts of flips and twirls as they dive.

The gradient eases considerably as you reach a rusty old fencepost. The path continues to a tumbledown wall. Walk with this on your left and you'll soon reach a cairn. Continue with the wall on your left on a reasonably clear path through the grass. The path drops slightly before climbing towards **Stony Cove Pike**. At the top of the climb, there's a grand view west – across to Crinkle Crags, Bow Fell and the Scafell range.

Continue along the flat, grassy summit area – still with the wall on your left – until you see a narrow trail crossing your path. Turn left here, crossing the wall to reach the cairn on Stony Cove Pike, the highest point of **Caudale Moor**. Turn left again along a clear path that soon reaches a wall. You now descend beside this wall: gently at first, but then on steep, rocky ground that requires care. The sweeping ridge of Froswick and Ill Bell can be seen to the south, and Windermere and Morecambe Bay also come into view soon. To cut the walk short, turn left on reaching Threshthwaite Mouth to drop to a clear path beside Pasture Beck. This leads back into Hartsop.

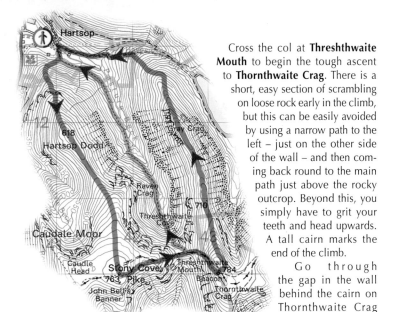

Cross the col at **Threshthwaite Mouth** to begin the tough ascent to **Thornthwaite Crag**. There is a short, easy section of scrambling on loose rock early in the climb, but this can be easily avoided by using a narrow path to the left – just on the other side of the wall – and then coming back round to the main path just above the rocky outcrop. Beyond this, you simply have to grit your teeth and head upwards. A tall cairn marks the end of the climb.

Go through the gap in the wall behind the cairn on Thornthwaite Crag and turn left. Walk with the wall on your left for about 150m and then, when it starts swinging left, keep straight ahead on a path along the top of the lonely **Gray Crag** ridge (north).

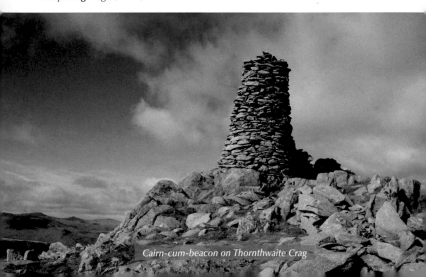

Cairn-cum-beacon on Thornthwaite Crag

Ridge path on Gray Crag

Across the valley to the left are **Raven Crag** and Hartsop Dodd; the steep slopes on the right lead up to High Street. As the ridge path starts descending, you can also see Hayeswater below to your right.

The path heads straight down the north ridge at first, but then swings right as you encounter steeper ground. Eventually, the path swings back to the left to cut under the crags that interrupted your direct descent. It becomes fainter as it heads north-west and then drops to a wide, stony track, along which you swing left. This crosses **Hayeswater Gill** and eventually leads back to Hartsop.

Hartsop, now a quiet hamlet, was once a busy industrial village. There were two mines in the area. The remains of Low Hartsop lead mine can be seen as you return to Hartsop. When you pass the confluence of Hayeswater Gill and Pasture Beck, you'll see the stone piers that formed part of the huge water wheel used to drain the mine. The works were abandoned in 1878.

Walk 27

High Street and Harter Fell

The ascent of High Street (828m) via Rough Crag and Long Stile passes through what is probably the finest mountain scenery in the far eastern fells. This ridge route is just narrow and rocky enough to excite walkers, but not enough to cause difficulties in normal weather conditions. After reaching the summit, the route drops to Mardale Ill Bell (761m) and Nan Bield Pass, an atmospheric, rocky gap high above the Kentmere valley. One final pull leads on to Harter Fell (778m) and, from here, there is a long, but straightforward descent to Gatescarth Pass and then Haweswater.

Haweswater from the Rough Crag ridge

Start/finish	Mardale Head car park at S end of Haweswater (NY 469 107)
Distance	10.5km (6½ miles)
Total ascent	795m (2610ft)
Grade	2
Walking time	4½hrs
Terrain	Open fell, mostly grassy; some rocky ground, including ridge; rough track on descent
Maps	OS Explorer OL5 and OL7; or OS Landranger 90
Refreshments	Haweswater Hotel; Mardale Inn and Bampton Village Store tearoom in Bampton
Transport	None

Go through the tall gates at the road-end and walk up the wide path. Where it splits at a wall corner, turn right to walk with the wall on your right – signposted Riggindale. Having crossed one small footbridge, cross Mardale Beck via a wider bridge and turn right on a path running along the base of the fell.

You'll have a wall on your right at first. Then, gradually, the path swings left – over the eastern end of **The Rigg**. The wall and the views over the southern end of the reservoir are now replaced by a conifer plantation.

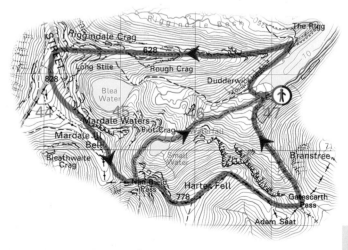

A few paces beyond a gap in a wall, take a trail through the bracken on the left. This follows the line of an old wall riding the crest of the ridge. As the path goes through a gap in an intervening wall, the ridge ahead suddenly rears up steeply. The route swings left here, across to the south side of the ridge wall, and finds an easier way on to the higher ground.

After a steep section, you're briefly reunited with the wall. The path then narrows, with steep drops to the left, before climbing back to the wall. The uphill journey now alternates between pleasant, grassy ridge and easy, rocky clambering on bare bedrock.

BIRDS OF PREY

England's last golden eagle nests on the slopes to the north of Rough Crag on the ridge route on to High Street. Eagles have called this valley home since 1969, and have fledged 16 young in that time. The current resident arrived in 2001, but his mate disappeared in 2004. One of the best times for trying to spot him is late winter and early spring when he performs his usual mating display flights and starts rebuilding his eyrie in preparation for the nesting season.

The Lake District is home to a variety of other birds of prey too. A pair of osprey made the shores of Bassenthwaite Lake their home in 2001. You've a chance of spotting these magnificent fish-eating birds on the Skiddaw route (Walk 1). Watch for their white or slightly mottled underparts. The long wings are angled and have a distinctive black patch that contrasts with the white wing linings.

Another reintroduced species is the red kite. Ninety birds were released in Grizedale Forest between 2010 and 2012. With their deeply forked tails, angled wings and reddish-brown colouring, these large but amazingly graceful birds are unmistakeable in flight.

Watch too for peregrine falcons with their distinctive yellow beaks and talons. Nesting on crags throughout the Lake District, these impressive raptors are just about the fastest creatures on the planet, said to be able to fly at speeds in excess of 160kmph when in pursuit of prey.

The wall disappears after a particularly tough, rocky clamber. The top of Rough Crag – at 628m, the highest point on this part of the ridge – is marked by a small cairn.

Drop to Caspel Gate, home to a tiny tarn. The only obstacle now standing between you and High Street is the steep ridge of **Long Stile**. As you ascend – with Blea Water twinkling in the sunshine on your left – you'll encounter one or two

Looking up Long Stile

rocky sections, but these are hardly any more difficult than those experienced on the Rough Crag ridge. In fact, the worst part of the ascent is the last few metres, beyond the rock outcrops, where you face a loose, stony path – just the sort of thing you could do without at the end of an ascent. The top of the climb is marked by a large cairn. Bear left (south-west) along a wide path to cross the flat, grassy plateau. Turn left at the wall and follow it to the trig point on top of **High Street**.

The **views** from here are pretty special. Filling the horizon to the north-west is the long, craggy ridge of the Helvellyn range. Further south you can see the Scafell range, Bow Fell, Crinkle Crags and the Coniston Fells. Further south still is Windermere; and to the east are the Pennines.

Harter Fell

Continue with the wall on your right for about 300m and then turn left along a constructed path that makes for easy walking almost all the way to the top of **Mardale Ill Bell**. From this nondescript summit, the path drops to **Nan Bield Pass**, a dramatic gap in the ridge with an eagle-eye view of Small Water directly below and Haweswater to the north-east. The hause itself, one of the highest of the major Lake District passes, is home to a substantial shelter. To cut the walk short, turn left at the shelter in Nan Bield Pass and descend to Mardale via Small Water.

From the shelter, continue uphill to **Harter Fell**. Keep to the clearest path, straight up the rocky front of the fell, and you'll come to the summit, marked by

a cairn with bits of metal sticking out of it. The panorama to the north-east now includes Cross Fell, the highest point on the Pennines.

Bear left from the cairn to walk with the fence on your right. Keep close to the fence after the next cairn too. As the fence turns sharp right, you suddenly find yourself on a constructed path. This continues beside the fence for a few more hundred metres and then swings left and drops to a track at **Gatescarth Pass**. Turn left here. The track makes for a steep and stony descent, but the setting is impressive: with the dark crags of Harter Fell looming to the west, you are able to enjoy views back across to Rough Crag and up towards the eastern corries of High Street and its neighbours. Bear right at a path junction to return to the car park at the road-end.

Walk 28

A Martindale Round

Is there a better way to start a walk than to catch the 'steamer' across glorious Ullswater? Embarking at Glenridding, you alight at Howtown and then head up Steel Knotts (432m), immediately immersing yourself in unfrequented fell country. A glorious array of grassy ridges is set around the lonely dale of Martindale. Making your way on to the Roman road, you then follow the broad, peaty crest of the fells – more akin to the Pennines than to the Lake District – to High Raise. At 802m, this is the highest point on the walk. Beyond Rampsgill Head (792m), the nature of the outing changes: the solitude of the ridge is lost as you join the route of Wainwright's Coast to Coast walk and follow a well-used path over Satura Crag, past Angle Tarn and down to Patterdale. Keep your binoculars handy at all times because there's a good chance of spotting red deer.

Kidsty Pike from near High Raise

Start	Ullswater Steamer pier in Howtown (NY 443 199)
Finish	Ullswater Steamer pier car park in Glenridding (NY 389 169)
Distance	17km (10½ miles)
Total ascent	860m (2820ft)
Grade	3
Walking time	6hrs
Terrain	Mostly grassy, open fell with a few damp, peaty patches
Maps	OS Explorer OL5; or OS Landranger 90
Refreshments	Choice of pubs and cafés in Glenridding
Transport	Ullswater 'Steamer' from Glenridding to Howtown (017684 82229; www.ullswater-steamers.co.uk)

Having caught the steamer from Glenridding, get off at Howtown and turn right at the end of the pier to cross the wooden footbridge – signposted Sandwick. When you reach an asphalt lane, turn left and then go straight across a minor road. You now enter the isolated hamlet of **Howtown**. Keep straight ahead on the lane between the buildings and then follow it gently uphill, keeping right at a fork.

map continues on page 187

After crossing a cattle grid, turn right along a grassy path beside a wall – signposted Martindale Hause. After about 100m, watch for a small rock outcrop to the left. Immediately after this, turn left along a very faint, easy-to-miss trail climbing the northeast ridge of **Steel Knotts**. Although the ascent is only short, it's steep in places, some of it making use of grassy rakes between the crags. A cairn marks the first summit about 800m into the climb. From here, stride out along the gorgeous ridge towards the

Ascending Steel Knotts

tor-like rocks marking the true summit, known as **Pikeawassa**.

From here, the head of **Bannerdale** looks a lonely, forlorn place while the rough slopes of Rampsgill Head seem harsh and uninviting. To your left are the steep, eastern slopes of Fusedale, rising towards Loadpot Hill, while the scene to the right includes Beda Fell and Place Fell. You may not have climbed much, but the scenery is truly magnificent.

Beyond the top, continue in roughly the same direction, descending to a wall. Cross this via a well-camouflaged stile, and then walk with the wall on your left. The path forks on a number of occasions: keeping close to the wall will ensure ease of navigation in mist, but means you have to climb every lump and bump on the ridge. Eventually, about 1.1km after the stile, you'll recross the wall via a wet gap. If you chose the right-hand route along the ridge, the path swings left across very damp ground to the north of **Gowk Hill** to reach this gap.

Having walked through the gap, pass a ruined building, ford a beck and immediately turn right along a narrow trail heading upstream. (This is just before a second, larger ruin.) This trail soon joins a slightly clearer path from the left. This later swings right (south-west) to recross the beck before winding its way up the grassy hillside (south-east). Unlike the steep right-of-way shown on OS maps, the actual path cuts across the western face of Wether Hill via a grassy groove and then climbs beside **Mere Beck**.

Eventually, with a tumbledown wall on the right, you reach a broad path along which you turn right. About 60m along this, bear right to cross the wall and follow the clear, but often damp and peaty path across the top of **Red Crag**. The extensive distant skyline to the left takes in much of the North Pennines, including Cross Fell, the highest point in England outside of the Lake District.

Before long, you'll see a fence to the right. The path and fence carry on in unison for a few hundred metres and then the path swings slightly left, closer to the wall, passing the circular Redcrag Tarn. Go through a small, wooden gate in a fence and then continue along the ridge – beside the wall on the left.

The impressive views to the right include Rest Dodd and The Nab directly across Ramps Gill. This forms part of Martindale's ancient **deer forest**. If you can't see red deer on its eastern slopes, there's a better chance you'll spot them from the other side.

Cross a wooden stile at the wall-end and head right – uphill, beside the fence. A clearer path then swings away from a small gate in the fence (south south-west).

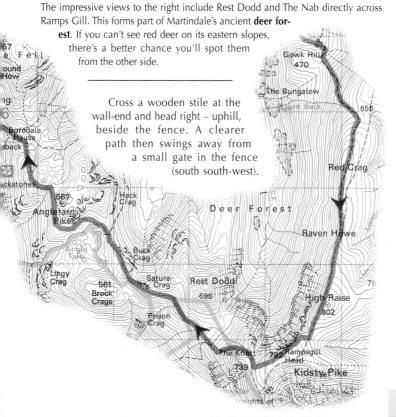

Roughly following the route of the Roman road known as High Street, this passes just to the right of the summit cairn on **High Raise**. The views west are improving all the while; as well as the Helvellyn range and Fairfield, more of the central fells can be seen now. Closer in is Ramps Gill's dramatic dalehead.

IN THE FOOTSTEPS OF THE ROMANS

The Roman road reaches its highest point as it crosses the fell today known as High Street

Nearly 2000 years ago, the Romans built a high-level road across the Lake District's eastern fells, linking their forts at Galava (Ambleside) and Brovacum (Brougham, near Penrith). This is known today as High Street, and, reaching a high point of about 800m on the fell now called High Street, it was the highest Roman road in the country. Little archaeological work has been carried out along the route, but at least one recent survey (TC Bell, 2011) suggests the route consisted of two parallel roadways, each about 5m wide. The same survey also discovered fortlets along the route, a number of 'minor roads' feeding into the main highway and evidence of the mineral sites that High Street exploited. Most of the 40km route is still used as a bridleway.

Cumbria was on the north-western edge of the mighty Roman Empire. The invaders had arrived in Britain in AD43, primarily to exploit the country's rich and varied mineral sources. Because of its strategic position on the edge of empire, Cumbria was mostly a military zone. The 20th-century historian Professor RG Collingwood once described the county as being "almost at vanishing point in the scale of Romanisation". As such, although there is plenty of evidence of Roman roads, such as High Street, forts and other defensive structures, you won't find villas or markets or even Roman place names. But the military establishment was an impressive one and many of the structures it built survive today.

The path splits as it drops to a shallow saddle. Take the first ascending path on the right (south-west). A few metres up from the saddle, take a faint, stony trail to the right, allowing a more intimate view of Rampsgill Head's crags and shattered rock pinnacles. A few strides beyond the cairn on top of **Rampsgill Head**, strike off right along a less-travelled path (west veering south-west). Turn right on dropping to a stony path near a wall – the route of Wainwright's Coast to Coast walk. This swings around the side of **The Knott** and descends a loose, stony section. At the bottom of this, bear right at a fork.

Having crossed a peaty area, largely on a constructed path, the route negotiates rock outcrops near **Satura Crag**. Keep reasonably close to the drystone wall/fence on the left here. Once past the rocky area, take some time to train your binoculars on the western slopes of Rest Dodd, a favourite haunt of red deer.

You'll soon see Angle Tarn below. Don't be tempted by a trail heading right as the clear path swings left, ascending slightly, on the northern side of the tarn. Instead, keep straight on and, before long, the ground on your left falls away, revealing jaw-dropping views down the steep slopes into the upper reaches of Patterdale and across to lonely Deepdale. This superb path hugs the edge of the fell and then drops to an unnaturally flat, grassy area at **Boredale Hause**. Continue in roughly the same direction, keeping to the right of Stonebarrow Gill.

At a fork, take either path: both strands meet up again later and drop to a junction above some cottages at **Rooking**. Turn left here and descend to a large gate.

Go through the gate and turn right, through another gate, to access a farm track. Reaching Side Farm, turn left between the buildings and follow the track across the meadows. Turn right at the main road. There are roadside paths all the way back to Glenridding – sometimes to the right of the asphalt, sometimes to the left. As you cross back to the eastern side of the road close to St Patrick's Landing, go through the small metal gate to pick up the lakeside path. This eventually emerges on a lane at the entrance to the Glenridding pier car park.

Angle Tarn

Walk 29

Place Fell and Beda Fell

Both Place Fell (657m) and Beda Fell (509m) fall into the 'mid-level' category of fells, and yet combining them creates a superb and surprisingly tough route. There are spectacular views to be had from the top of the higher fell, while the latter provides a wonderful, roller-coaster ride and a great sense of solitude. Rejecting the tourist route on to Place Fell, this walk climbs the less well-known Hare Shaw path up the fell's juniper-covered front. From the summit, it heads north-east before dropping into Boredale and then climbing again on to Beda Fell. The descent at the end of the day is from Boredale Hause.

Place Fell from Beda Fell

Start/finish	George Starkey Hut, Patterdale (NY 394 160). There is room for a few cars to park in front of the building. Alternatively, the pay-and-display car park is 200m to the SE.
Distance	12.9km (8 miles)
Total ascent	935m (3070ft)
Grade	2/3
Walking time	5½hrs
Terrain	Mostly grassy, open fell
Maps	OS Explorer OL5; or OS Landranger 90
Refreshments	White Lion Inn and the Patterdale Hotel, both in Patterdale
Transport	Bus 508

Take the track beside the George Starkey Hut in Patterdale. This goes through the yard at Side Farm. Turn left around the back of the buildings to join a wide track. Immediately after the gate, turn right to climb beside the wall on the right for just a few metres. Then, very quickly, bear left to climb the steep, grassy slope. On reaching a clearer path in a short while, turn left. This soon passes some open quarry workings and an old green bench. You couldn't ask for a better start to a walk than this superb balcony path with its excellent views across Ullswater to Grisedale and the Helvellyn range.

About 800m beyond the green bench, take the grassy path heading up to the right. With juniper encroaching, this gets steeper and rockier as you gain height, but never requires hands. If you turn round now, be prepared for a shock: that wonderful view you were enjoying earlier just got even better. As the gradient eases, the path swings right. After passing

Ullswater from the balcony path at the start of the walk

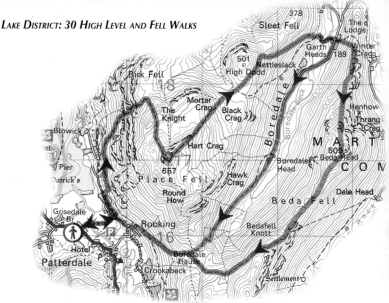

through a shallow
gap, you reach a confluence of two tiny becks. The path forks here. Bear right,
crossing the smaller of the becks. The trick now is not to lose the path as it winds
its way uphill between rocky knolls. The general direction is south-east. If you lose
the path, keep to the fell's western rim; the trig pillar is perched on a jagged lump
of rock just a few metres back from this edge.

Just before reaching the summit of **Place Fell** – and its splendid views of the
Helvellyn range – you'll come up on to a much clearer path. The trig pillar is
about 60m up to the right, but the main route goes left. Having turned your back
on the high, craggy fells, the outlook is now softer and more rounded, with the
North Pennines in the distance.The path passes to the left of a small tarn and
later drops, via some badly eroded sections, to an old sheepfold. Crossing boggy
ground here, keep right to curve round the southern flank of **High Dodd**.

About 800m beyond the sheepfold, as the gently descending path levels off,
turn right. A sunken path zig-zags its way steeply down the grassy fellside. In no
time at all, you find yourself directly above a stone barn near **Garth Heads** in
Boredale. Take the next path on the right and then turn left to drop to a stile above
the barn. Cross this and then a second stile on your right. Head down the field,
keeping close to the wall on your left.

After the barn, swing right along the rough track. After the gate at the bottom,
cross the footbridge just upstream of the ford over **Boredale Beck**. Swing left up

Bridge across Boredale Beck

the grassy slope to rejoin the track, which leads to a minor road. To cut the walk short by omitting Beda Fell, turn right along the road. It later becomes a rough track leading up to Boredale Hause where you rejoin the main walk description.

Cross the road and climb the stile in the fence opposite. A grassy path heads uphill between two walls. When you lose the walls, keep heading straight up the fell. You finally reach the ridge close to a bench. Turn right along the ridge path.

Beda Fell is mostly grassy, but there are a few rocky interludes to add some spice to the experience. The views are of Martindale to the left and Boredale to the right, remote valleys that see few visitors. After a dip in the ridge, the climb on to **Beda Head** begins. About a third of the way up this slope, you reach a fork. Take either branch: the one on the left is easier, but the one on the right keeps to the ridge proper. The paths have a reunion of sorts at a boggy area just below a large cairn, but then both dissolve into the mire. Continue uphill to reach the small cairn that marks the highest point on the fell. Helvellyn and its neighbours reappear now. Over to the left are The Nab and Rest Dodd, the main haunt of Martindale's red deer.

THE RED DEER RUT

Martindale is home to England's oldest native herd of red deer, said to be the only herd that hasn't cross-bred with sika deer. The ancient deer forest itself is centred on The Nab, but the deer range all over these fells and into neighbouring Mardale and Kentmere. If you walk Place Fell and Beda Fell in the autumn, particularly in the early morning or late evening, you may hear an eerie noise: like a cross between the deep mooing of cows and the rumble of distant trail bikes, it is in fact the sound of the deer rutting. This deep bellowing means the stags, who congregate in single-sex herds for much of the year, have gone their separate ways and are now gathering their individual harems for the mating season. The roar performs two functions. Firstly, the loudest and most frequent wins the females. Secondly, it forms part of the posturing used by a male to achieve dominance over other stags. Another element of this is the antler fight, during which the animals lock antlers and attempt to push each other away. The strongest secures hinds for mating.

The rut lasts about six weeks, during which time stags will patrol their harems chasing off any rival stags that come near and ensuring their hinds, numbering as many as 40, are not tempted to stray. At the end of this period, the stags, often emaciated from such an energetic few weeks, leave the females. The young are born from mid-May to July.

A rough path descends from Boredale Hause

The ridge path continues in its undulating fashion. About 1.6km beyond the cairn on Beda Head, turn right at a crossing of paths marked by a cairn. With impressive views of St Sunday Crag on the other side of Patterdale, this excellent path weaves its gentle way down to **Boredale Hause**.

Keep left at a faint fork just above the pass, continuing roughly west north-west across a boggy patch. Having reached an unnaturally flat, grassy area where a number of paths meet, continue in roughly the same direction, keeping to the right of Stonebarrow Gill. At a fork, take either path: both strands meet up again later and drop to a junction above some cottages at **Rooking**. Turn left here and descend to a large gate. Go through the gate and turn right, through another gate, to access a farm track. Reaching Side Farm, turn left between the buildings and retrace your steps to the George Starkey Hut.

Walk 30

Matterdale and The Dodds

Broad, grassy ridges with far-reaching views are the order of the day on this long walk to the north-west of Ullswater. After a gentle amble up through the spectacular Aira Gorge and a long section of road and moorland track walking, the route climbs to Clough Head (726m), Great Dodd (856m), Watson's Dodd (789m), Stybarrow Dodd (843m) and White Stones (795m). These aren't difficult hills in themselves but, climbed together and combined with the long walk-in, they make for a reasonably hard day on the fells. There are more Lakeland glories to be enjoyed even after dropping from the tops: wild Glencoyne, a superb view of Ullswater and the delightful path back across Glencoyne Park.

Looking back towards Calfhow Pike with Skiddaw behind

Start/finish	Small car park above Aira Force on east side of A5091 (NY 397 205), 1.4km S of Dockray
Distance	22.2km (13¾ miles)
Total ascent	1000m (3280ft)
Grade	3/4
Walking time	7¾hrs
Terrain	Good path through gorge; quiet roads; rough track; open fell, mostly grassy but boggy in places
Maps	OS Explorer OL5; or OS Landranger 90
Refreshments	Royal Hotel, Dockray
Transport	Bus 508 runs along the nearby A592.

Take the clear path through the trees from the bottom end of the car park. After the first gate, keep straight ahead, over a bridge. Follow the path left to a gate, beyond which you turn left.

Take the second set of steps on the right, crossing the bridge over the top of **Aira Force**. Turn left along the beckside path, heading upstream and later joining another path from the right.

Having left the woods and passed through two gates, you ford a small beck. Keep to the wide track. Having crossed a bridge, climb to a T-junction close to Aira Beck and turn right. Reaching the road in **Dockray**, cross diagonally left to pass in front of the Royal Hotel – along a minor road signposted High Row and Dowthwaite Head.

After about 1.5km of road walking, cross straight over at a junction to walk along a gravel track. This quickly goes through a gate – signposted St John's in the Vale. Follow the broad, stony track, known as the **Old Coach Road**, out across open moorland for just over 5km. Along the way, it fords

Mosedale

Groove Beck, passes beneath **Wolf Crags**, crosses Mariel Bridge over **Mosedale Beck** and then slowly climbs. Nearing the brow of the hill, with good views across to Blencathra, you pass a tin-roofed building. About 50m beyond this, go through the gate in the fence on the left.

A moderately steep, narrow path heads up the grassy slope (south-west, swinging south). At the top of the first rise, you have the cairn-topped mound of White Pike to your left. Bear right here to continue climbing to **Clough Head**.

The summit is marked by a trig pillar, which enjoys views of practically all the major fells to the west of the A591 (see Walk 6 for a full description). You'll see two paths heading away from the trig point. Take the one on the left (south-west, veering south as it descends). The grassy track, boggy in places, splits just before the small, rocky knoll of **Calfhow Pike**. Bear right to climb to the top, or keep left to bypass it. Escape routes are few on this long walk. However, it is possible to regain the Old Coach Road by heading north-east through Mosedale just after passing Calfhow Pike. Alternatively, descend north-east from the top of Great Dodd, crossing very boggy ground along the way and following Groove Beck back to the track.

The clear path then climbs **Great Dodd**, disappearing just before the summit; maintain your bearing and you'll soon reach the cairn at the top. Continuing south-east from the summit cairn, you reach a large shelter. Head south south-west to pick up a clear path along the wide, grassy ridge. Just over 300m beyond the shelter, you will see a choice of paths crossing the fell-top ahead. To reach the top of **Watson's Dodd**, take the one furthest right; to bypass it, choose the one on the left. If you go out to the summit cairn, you will need to follow the grassy path south-east to regain the main route.

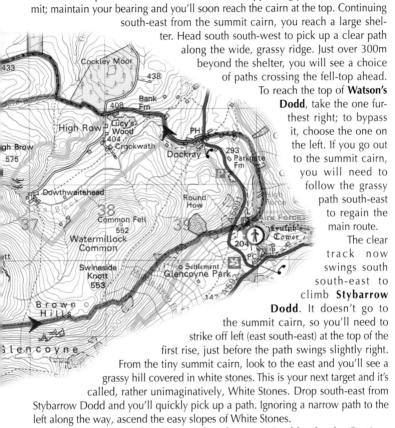

The clear track now swings south south-east to climb **Stybarrow Dodd**. It doesn't go to the summit cairn, so you'll need to strike off left (east south-east) at the top of the first rise, just before the path swings slightly right. From the tiny summit cairn, look to the east and you'll see a grassy hill covered in white stones. This is your next target and it's called, rather unimaginatively, White Stones. Drop south-east from Stybarrow Dodd and you'll quickly pick up a path. Ignoring a narrow path to the left along the way, ascend the easy slopes of White Stones.

The first cairn on White Stones is found among a jumble of rocks. Continue east to a second and then third cairn. Now drop south-east, soon picking up a narrow trail. When this forks, keep left, passing some way above the crumbly edge of a large, dangerous quarry pit. As the northern end of Ullswater comes into view, the descent, still on grass, steepens.

On reaching a crossing of paths, turn left. A superb path now traverses the headwall of magnificent **Glencoyne**, a wild, little-visited valley – with steep slopes plunging away to the right.

Having crossed one drystone wall via an awkward stile, you gradually drop towards another wall. The stunning vista ahead is a surprisingly rare sight: almost the entire length of glorious Ullswater is visible. Having walked beside the wall for about 150m, go through a small gate in it – the main path comes away from

A view of Ullswater and the Eastern Fells from the path above Glencoyne

the wall slightly here, so this right turn is easily missed. A faint path drops east north-east, battling through high bracken in summer. It eventually leads back to the A5091, directly opposite the car park where the walk started.

APPENDIX A

Useful contacts

Tourist Information Centres
Bowness-on-Windermere
Glebe Road
Bowness-on-Windermere
LA23 3HJ
Tel: 0845 901 0845

Keswick
Moot Hall
Keswick
CA12 5JR
Tel: 0845 901 0845

Ullswater
Beckside Car Park
Glenridding
Penrith
CA11 0PD
Tel: 017684 82414

Ambleside
Central Buildings
Market Cross
Ambleside
LA22 9BS
Tel: 015394 32582

Coniston
Ruskin Avenue
Coniston
LA21 8EH
Tel: 015394 41533

Other useful sources of information
Lake District Weatherline

Tel: 0844 846 2444
www.lakedistrictweatherline.co.uk

Mountain Weather Information Service
www.mwis.org.uk

Cumbria Tourism
www.visitlakedistrict.com

Traveline
Tel: 0871 200 2233
www.traveline.org.uk

Fix The Fells
www.fixthefells.co.uk

Glencoyne Head

Gimmer Crag, popular with climbers, towers above Great Langdale (walk 17)

LISTING OF CICERONE GUIDES

BRITISH ISLES CHALLENGES, COLLECTIONS AND ACTIVITIES

Cycling Land's End to John o' Groats
The Big Rounds
The Book of the Bothy
The C2C Cycle Route
The End to End Cycle Route
The Mountains of England and Wales: Vol 1 Wales
The Mountains of England and Wales: Vol 2 England
The National Trails
Walking The End to End Trail

SCOTLAND

Backpacker's Britain: Northern Scotland
Ben Nevis and Glen Coe
Cycle Touring in Northern Scotland
Cycling in the Hebrides
Great Mountain Days in Scotland
Mountain Biking in Southern and Central Scotland
Mountain Biking in West and North West Scotland
Not the West Highland Way Scotland
Scotland's Best Small Mountains
Scotland's Mountain Ridges
Skye's Cuillin Ridge Traverse
The Ayrshire and Arran Coastal Paths
The Borders Abbeys Way
The Great Glen Way
The Great Glen Way Map Booklet
The Hebridean Way
The Hebrides
The Isle of Mull
The Isle of Skye
The Skye Trail
The Southern Upland Way
The Speyside Way
The Speyside Way Map Booklet
The West Highland Way
The West Highland Way Map Booklet
Walking Highland Perthshire
Walking in the Cairngorms
Walking in the Pentland Hills
Walking in the Scottish Borders
Walking in the Southern Uplands
Walking in Torridon
Walking Loch Lomond and the Trossachs
Walking on Arran
Walking on Harris and Lewis
Walking on Jura, Islay and Colonsay
Walking on Rum and the Small Isles
Walking on the Orkney and Shetland Isles
Walking on Uist and Barra
Walking the Cape Wrath Trail
Walking the Corbetts
Vol 1 South of the Great Glen
Vol 2 North of the Great Glen
Walking the Galloway Hills
Walking the Munros
Vol 1 – Southern, Central and Western Highlands
Vol 2 – Northern Highlands and the Cairngorms
Winter Climbs Ben Nevis and Glen Coe
Winter Climbs in the Cairngorms

NORTHERN ENGLAND TRAILS

Hadrian's Wall Path
Hadrian's Wall Path Map Booklet
The Coast to Coast Walk
The Coast to Coast Walk Map Booklet
The Dales Way
The Dales Way Map Booklet
The Pennine Way
The Pennine Way Map Booklet
Walking the Tour of the Lake District

NORTH EAST ENGLAND, YORKSHIRE DALES AND PENNINES

Cycling in the Yorkshire Dales
Great Mountain Days in the Pennines
Mountain Biking in the Yorkshire Dales
St Oswald's Way and St Cuthbert's Way
The Cleveland Way and the Yorkshire Wolds Way
The Cleveland Way Map Booklet
The North York Moors
The Reivers Way
The Teesdale Way
Trail and Fell Running in the Yorkshire Dales
Walking in County Durham
Walking in Northumberland
Walking in the North Pennines
Walking in the Yorkshire Dales: North and East
Walking in the Yorkshire Dales: South and West

NORTH WEST ENGLAND THE ISLE OF MAN

Cycling the Pennine Bridleway
Cycling the Way of the Roses
Hadrian's Cycleway
Isle of Man Coastal Path
The Lancashire Cycleway
The Lune Valley and Howgills
Walking in Cumbria's Eden Valley
Walking in Lancashire
Walking in the Forest of Bowland and Pendle
Walking on the Isle of Man
Walking on the West Pennine Moors
Walks in Silverdale and Arnside

LAKE DISTRICT

Cycling in the Lake District
Great Mountain Days in the Lake District
Lake District Winter Climbs
Lake District: High Level and Fell Walks
Lake District: Low Level and Lake Walks
Mountain Biking in the Lake District
Outdoor Adventures with Children – Lake District
Scrambles in the Lake District – North
Scrambles in the Lake District – South
The Cumbria Way
Trail and Fell Running in the Lake District
Walking the Lake District Fells:
Borrowdale
Buttermere
Coniston
Keswick
Langdale
Mardale and the Far East
Patterdale
Wasdale

DERBYSHIRE, PEAK DISTRICT AND MIDLANDS

Cycling in the Peak District
Dark Peak Walks
Scrambles in the Dark Peak
Walking in Derbyshire
Walking in the Peak District – White Peak East

SOUTHERN ENGLAND

20 Classic Sportive Rides in South East England
20 Classic Sportive Rides in South West England

Cycling in the Cotswolds
Mountain Biking on the North Downs
Mountain Biking on the South Downs
Suffolk Coast and Heath Walks
The Cotswold Way
The Cotswold Way Map Booklet
The Great Stones Way
The Kennet and Avon Canal
The Lea Valley Walk
The North Downs Way
The North Downs Way Map Booklet
The Peddars Way and Norfolk Coast Path
The Pilgrims' Way
The Ridgeway Map Booklet
The Ridgeway National Trail
The South Downs Way
The South Downs Way Map Booklet
The Thames Path
The Thames Path Map Booklet
The Two Moors Way
The Two Moors Way Map Booklet
Walking Hampshire's Test Way
Walking in Cornwall
Walking in Essex
Walking in Kent
Walking in London
Walking in Norfolk
Walking in the Chilterns
Walking in the Cotswolds
Walking in the Isles of Scilly
Walking in the New Forest
Walking in the North Wessex Downs
Walking in the Thames Valley
Walking on Dartmoor
Walking on Guernsey
Walking on Jersey
Walking on the Isle of Wight
Walking the Jurassic Coast
Walking the South West Coast Path
Walking the South West Coast Path Map Booklets:
Vol 1: Minehead to St Ives
Vol 2: St Ives to Plymouth
Vol 3: Plymouth to Poole
Walks in the South Downs National Park

WALES AND WELSH BORDERS

Cycle Touring in Wales
Cycling Lon Las Cymru
Glyndwr's Way
Great Mountain Days in Snowdonia
Hillwalking in Shropshire
Hillwalking in Wales – Vols 1& 2
Mountain Walking in Snowdonia
Offa's Dyke Path

Offa's Dyke Path Map Booklet
Ridges of Snowdonia
Scrambles in Snowdonia
Snowdonia: 30 Low-level and easy walks – North
Snowdonia: 30 Low-level and easy walks – South
The Cambrian Way
The Ceredigion and Snowdonia Coast Paths
The Pembrokeshire Coast Path
The Pembrokeshire Coast Path Map Booklet
The Severn Way
The Snowdonia Way
The Wales Coast Path
The Wye Valley Walk
Walking in Carmarthenshire
Walking in Pembrokeshire
Walking in the Forest of Dean
Walking in the Wye Valley
Walking on the Brecon Beacons
Walking on the Gower
Walking the Shropshire Way

INTERNATIONAL CHALLENGES, COLLECTIONS AND ACTIVITIES

Canyoning in the Alps
Europe's High Points

AFRICA

Kilimanjaro
The High Atlas
Walking in the Drakensberg
Walks and Scrambles in the Moroccan Anti-Atlas

ALPS CROSS-BORDER ROUTES

100 Hut Walks in the Alps
Alpine Ski Mountaineering Vol 1 – Western Alps
Alpine Ski Mountaineering Vol 2 – Central and Eastern Alps
Chamonix to Zermatt
The Karnischer Hohenweg
The Tour of the Bernina
Tour of Monte Rosa
Tour of the Matterhorn
Trail Running – Chamonix and the Mont Blanc region
Trekking in the Alps
Trekking in the Silvretta and Ratikon Alps
Trekking Munich to Venice
Trekking the Tour of Mont Blanc
Walking in the Alps

PYRENEES AND FRANCE/SPAIN CROSS-BORDER ROUTES

Shorter Treks in the Pyrenees
The GR10 Trail
The GR11 Trail
The Pyrenean Haute Route
The Pyrenees
Walks and Climbs in the Pyrenees

AUSTRIA

Innsbruck Mountain Adventures
The Adlerweg
Trekking in Austria's Hohe Tauern
Trekking in the Stubai Alps
Trekking in the Zillertal Alps
Walking in Austria
Walking in the Salzkammergut: the Austrian Lake District

EASTERN EUROPE

The Danube Cycleway Vol 2
The High Tatras
The Mountains of Romania
Walking in Bulgaria's National Parks
Walking in Hungary

FRANCE, BELGIUM AND LUXEMBOURG

Chamonix Mountain Adventures
Cycle Touring in France
Cycling London to Paris
Cycling the Canal de la Garonne
Cycling the Canal du Midi
Mont Blanc Walks
Mountain Adventures in the Maurienne
Short Treks on Corsica
The GR20 Corsica
The GR5 Trail
The GR5 Trail – Benelux and Lorraine
The GR5 Trail – Vosges and Jura
The Grand Traverse of the Massif Central
The Loire Cycle Route
The Moselle Cycle Route
The River Rhone Cycle Route
The Way of St James – Le Puy to the Pyrenees
Tour of the Queyras
Trekking the Robert Louis Stevenson Trail
Vanoise Ski Touring
Via Ferratas of the French Alps
Walking in Corsica
Walking in Provence – East
Walking in Provence – West
Walking in the Ardennes
Walking in the Auvergne
Walking in the Brianconnais
Walking in the Dordogne
Walking in the Haute Savoie: North
Walking in the Haute Savoie: South

GERMANY

Hiking and Cycling in the Black Forest
The Danube Cycleway Vol 1
The Rhine Cycle Route
The Westweg
Walking in the Bavarian Alps

For full information on all our
guides, books and eBooks,
visit our website:
www.cicerone.co.uk.